Genesis
and
Archaeology

GENESIS
and
ARCHAEOLOGY

Howard F. Vos

Academie
Books Grand Rapids, Michigan
Zondervan Publishing House

GENESIS AND ARCHAEOLOGY
Copyright © 1985 by The Zondervan Corporation
Grand Rapids, Michigan

This is a revised and enlarged edition of *Genesis and Archaeology,* published
in 1963 by Moody Press.

ACADEMIE BOOKS is an imprint of Zondervan Publishing House,
1415 Lake Drive, S.E., Grand Rapids, Michigan 49506.

Library of Congress Cataloging in Publication Data

Vos, Howard Frederic, 1925–
    Genesis and archaeology.
    Bibliography: p.
    Includes index.
    1. Bible. O.T. Genesis—Antiquities.   I. Title.
BS1235.2.V6   1985   222'.11093   84-22032
ISBN 0-310-33901-4

Designed by Louise Bauer

Printed in the United States of America

85 86 87 88 89 90 / 10 9 8 7 6 5 4 3 2 1

To the memory of
Joseph P. Free
Beloved Mentor

CONTENTS

INTRODUCTION

Pick and spade have been unearthing the layer-cake civilizations of the ancient Near East for about a century and a half. Results have been overwhelming. Museum halls in Europe, America, and the Near East are well stocked with originals or casts of monuments, statues, clay tablets, and other artifacts the mounds have been forced to surrender. And the day of diminishing returns has not yet dawned. Chairs of Near Eastern studies have been established in many universities; in several of these schools a doctorate in one or more fields of Near Eastern studies is offered.

Of course, not all of the material discovered has a bearing on the study of Genesis. Much of it pertains to purely secular matters. Significant materials relate to other books of the Bible. But finds relating to Genesis are extensive—far too numerous for all of them to be even alluded to in a book of this size.

An archaeological commentary on individual verses of Genesis is therefore impossible here. Instead, several topics have been chosen in connection with the major divisions of the outline of Genesis. For instance, Mesopotamian creation accounts, the Babylonian sabbath, and the location of the Garden of Eden are discussed in relation to the first two chapters of the book.

It is not the responsibility of an archaeologist to deal with such tantalizing questions as the origin of man, the length of man's stay on earth, or the origin of the races. Such matters are properly the concern of the anthropologist. Most aspects of study about the Flood are the responsibility of the geologist. The problem of accounting for Jacob's streaked cattle (Gen. 31) involves the zoologist. Therefore, many questions the reader may have about Genesis are not discussed in this book.[1] It should be pointed out, however, that archaeology is a composite science that utilizes the findings of chemists, zoologists, botanists, anthropologists, hydrographers, and many others in arriving at conclusions about defunct civilizations.

Contrary to the belief of many who view an archaeologist as a morbid character interested in dead men's bones, the Near Eastern archaeologist concerns himself primarily with excavating the mounds of the Near East in an effort to reconstruct a picture of *life* as it was once lived there. While he concentrates on interpretation of the material remains of an ancient culture, he seeks also to gain some idea of the spiritual nature of the people who developed that culture. The biblical archaeologist tries to turn all this information to account in improving his knowledge of the contents of Scripture and its historical backgrounds. Sometimes he also uses his discoveries to support the veracity of the Bible.

---

[1] Some of these questions are dealt with briefly in the author's *Genesis*, published in the *Everyman's Bible Commentary Series* (Chicago: Moody Press, 1982).

Part I
THE EARLY
BEGINNINGS

GENESIS 1:1–11:30

1 | *CREATION*
Genesis 1–2

Near Eastern archaeology was born in the cradles of war, commerce, and diplomacy. Napoleon was responsible for kindling the first extensive interest when he took nearly one hundred artists and scholars with him on his Egyptian campaign in 1798. Amazed at what they saw in the Nile Valley, those men passed on to Western scholarship copies of texts they discovered and descriptions of monuments they saw. During the campaign the Rosetta Stone, key to the decipherment of Egyptian hieroglyphics, was also found. Early in the following century, Claudius James Rich, representative of the British East India Company at Baghdad, aroused great interest in antiquities of Mesopotamia by rummaging among the mounds of ancient cities there and discovering many inscriptions. His memoirs on Babylon, Nineveh, and other Mesopotamian sites also contributed to popular fascination with archaeology. Then, in 1842, Paul Botta, a French vice-consul at Mosul (across the Tigris from Nineveh), began to excavate at Nineveh and subsequently worked extensively at nearby Khorsabad. At the latter location he found the palace of Sargon, conqueror of Samaria. So a military genius, a businessman, and a diplomat were responsible for the beginnings of Near Eastern archaeology.

THE BABYLONIAN CREATION ACCOUNT

Another diplomat was indirectly responsible for finding an ancient Babylonian creation account. Austen Henry Layard, a young Englishman destined for a diplomatic and political career, became fired with enthusiasm for a recovery of ancient civilizations. He began work at Nineveh in 1845, remaining until 1847. After his appointment as attaché to the British embassy in Constantinople (1849), he returned to his excavations in Mesopotamia. Associated with Layard was a native of Mosul named Hormuzd Rassam. To Rassam goes the credit for discovering in 1852 and 1853 the famous library of Ashurbanipal, king of Assyria from 668 to 626 B.C. Ashurbanipal had sent his scribes throughout Mesopotamia to copy and/or translate existing literature. He amassed a library of tens of thousands of clay tablets, among which was a copy of the Babylonian creation account, probably dating to the days of Hammurabi, king of Babylonia about 1700 B.C.

In the early days of excavation, large monuments and sculptures were much more sought after than clay tablets. Not only did the larger objects have more dramatic appeal but also translation was in its infancy. So it was not until 1876 that George Smith of the British Museum published some of the fragments of the creation account from Ashurbanipal's library. A few years later (1882) Rassam found a bilingual creation account, in Sumerian and Babylonian, at modern Abu-Habba (ancient Sippar), a few miles north of Babylon. Early in the the twentieth century, a German team working at Ashur (old capital of Assyria) discovered an Assyrian version of the Babylonian creation narrative. In the 1920s, portions of a Babylonian copy dating to the days of Nebuchadnezzar (c. 600 B.C.) were found at Kish and Uruk. From all of these materials it has been possible to restore the

Babylonian account of Ashurbanipal's library almost in its entirety.[1]

Immediately our curiosity is aroused. What does the *Enuma Elish* (the name by which the Babylonian account is known—so-called from its first two words) have to say about creation? How does it relate to the biblical account? Is there any evidence of borrowing in either direction?

The *Enuma Elish* consists of about one thousand lines of text on seven clay tablets. The contents of each tablet may be summarized as follows:

1. The narrative begins with the time when only Apsu (male personification of fresh water ocean) and Tiamat (female personification of primeval salt water ocean) existed. They begat or created a whole company of gods. These so tried the patience of Apsu that he determined to slay them all. But Ea (an early male descendant of the original pair of deities), after discovering the plan, bound and slew Apsu. Then Ea begat Marduk, later considered to be the patron god of Babylon. And Tiamat prepared to avenge the death of her husband. She created terrible monsters and placed Kingu at the head of her hosts.

2. Tablet 2 describes the counterplot of Ea against Tiamat and his search for a champion to oppose Tiamat. He appoints Marduk to the task.

3. Tablet 3 tells of a great banquet held in preparation for Marduk's entrance into battle.

4. According to tablet 4, Tiamat (chaos) and Marduk (the god of light) clash in ferocious combat. Marduk slew Tiamat, the conquest signifying the final victory of order over chaos, and from her body he created the heavens. Later he created the earth. Then he appointed residences for the gods of sky, air, and subterranean waters.

5. Tablet 5 is very fragmentary, but it has to do with

---

[1] Translations of the *Enuma Elish* may be found in Alexander Heidel, *The Babylonian Genesis,* 2nd ed. (Chicago: University of Chicago Press, 1951); George A. Barton, *Archaeology and the Bible,* 7th ed. (Philadelphia: American Sunday-School Union, 1937); and James G. Pritchard, ed., *Ancient Near Eastern Texts Relating to the Old Testament,* 2nd ed. (Princeton: Princeton University Press, 1954).

Marduk's appointment of the moon to rule over the night and to indicate the days and months of the year, and his formation of the constellations.

6. On tablet 6 appears Marduk's creation of man with the blood of Kingu, captain of Tiamat's host. The service of the gods is assigned as man's obligation. Then a great banquet is held in honor of Marduk.

7. Finally, according to tablet 7, Marduk was advanced from a position as chief god of Babylon to headship over all the gods.

The bilingual account discovered by Rassam in 1882 supplements *Enuma Elish* by giving Marduk and some of the other gods credit for creating grass, forests, rivers, and animals.

Looking at the above description and comparing it with the Genesis narrative of creation, one finds some interesting similarities. (1) Genesis speaks of seven days of creation; the Babylonian account was recorded on seven tablets. (2) Both describe a time when the earth was waste and void. (3) In Genesis, order follows chaos; in *Enuma Elish,* Marduk defeats chaos and establishes order. (4) Both accounts tell of the creation of moon, stars, plant life, animals, and man. (5) Man was created on the sixth day according to Genesis; *Enuma Elish* records man's creation on the sixth tablet.

But the differences are vastly greater. In the first place, *Enuma Elish* is not primarily a creation account. Its purpose is political: by portraying the preeminent place of her patron deity (Marduk) among the gods, to advance the cause of Babylon in her bid for supremacy. It is essentially a hymn to Marduk. It is interesting to note that the Assyrian version found by the Germans early in this century substituted the name of the Assyrian patron Ashur for Marduk. Genesis definitely sets forth a creation account. Second, *Enuma Elish* is grossly polytheistic; various gods share in the origin of things. Marduk himself is brought into existence by another god. Genesis posits an exalted monotheism with God as the creator of all things. Third, the gross mythology and inferior morals of *Enuma Elish* have no parallel in Genesis. Fourth, there is little parallel between the seven tablets and the seven creative days of Genesis. Tablets 2 and 3 do not deal with any phase of creation. Last, in starting its account of creation with the existence of matter, *Enuma Elish* implies eternity of matter; Scripture teaches that God is a spirit who is the author of all matter.

Though it is clear that the Genesis and Babylonian accounts of creation are far more different than similar, it still must be admitted that there are striking similarities. So scholars have struggled for years over the problem of relationship. A few have suggested that the Babylonians borrowed from the Bible and introduced pagan elements. But *Enuma Elish* and its antecedents date long before the writing of Genesis. Higher critics commonly have held that the biblical account is a purified version of the Babylonian. The differences in the two are almost too great to permit such a view, however.

Others have argued cogently that both came from a common inheritance. The various races of mankind possessed a knowledge of the events of creation. Among some peoples the narrative became more polluted than among others. The Genesis record represents the purest of these various accounts—one preserved by God Himself. It should be remembered that both *Enuma Elish* and the Genesis account come from the same area—an area where civilization began, according to both Genesis and the conclusions of archaeology. Possibly Abraham brought a creation account with him from Ur to Canaan. If so, it would then have been preserved by the Israelites until Moses recorded it in the Book of Genesis. A belief in a high view of inspiration does not require that God had to dictate a fresh statement of every event to the biblical writer; it merely guarantees that God preserved a given narrative or source from error. It is clear from many passages of Scripture that writers either made use of documents or did research in preparation for their writing. Note, for instance, the allusions in Joshua 10:13 and 2 Samuel 1:18 to the Book of Jasher and the research Luke did in preparation for the writing of his Gospel (Luke 1:1–4).

Whether or not there is any truth to the idea that the

Genesis account was preserved from time immemorial and passed on to Moses, it must be recognized that the differences between it and the Babylonian account are so great as to make the similarities shrivel into utter insignificance. The Genesis portrayal of a sovereign, omnipotent God who spoke the earth and everything on it into existence and created humankind in His image is without parallel in the known literature of the ancient Near East.

THE SABBATH

Genesis records that after God's activity on six creative days, "he rested on the seventh day from all his work which he had made." Later, God commanded Israel to observe the Sabbath as a day of rest (Exod. 20:10–11).

A Babylonian tablet that describes the nature of the days of the month has frequently been related to the Hebrew Sabbath. It set aside the seventh day as a feast to Marduk and Zarpanit and prohibited certain activities on that day.[2] In that same account, similar restrictions were placed on activities on the fourteenth, nineteenth, twenty-first, and twenty-eighth days. Other tablets indicate that special sacrifices were offered on the seventh, fourteenth, twenty-first, and twenty-eighth days of the month. It is interesting to note that none of these days is called a sabbath. But another tablet does call the fifteenth day of the month *shabatum,* etymologically equivalent to the Hebrew sabbath.

Several observations may be made in reply to those who would equate the biblical sabbath with the Babylonian observance of days that were multiples of seven or suggest that the Hebrews borrowed the concept of the sabbath from the Babylonians. Differences between the biblical and Babylonian observances are great. The Babylonians paid special attention to the nineteenth day as well as those that were multiples of seven; they called only the fifteenth day *shabatum.* The tablets call the seventh day "an evil day" or

---

[2]I. M. Price, O. R. Sellers, and E. Leslie Carlson, *The Monuments and the Old Testament* (Philadelphia: Judson Press, 1958), pp. 109–11.

"an unlucky day," whereas Scripture describes it as "a holy day." The Babylonians placed prohibitions only on the "king," "shepherd of the great peoples," "seer," and "the physician," whereas the Old Testament makes the sabbath binding on all. Again, in contrast to the Hebrew sabbath, there was no cessation of business activity on Babylonian special days. Last, though Babylonians had special regard for days that were multiples of seven, those days rarely ever fell on the seventh day of the week in their lunar calendar and thus were not equivalent to the Hebrew sabbath. It does not seem, therefore, that there was any necessary connection between the Hebrew sabbath and Babylonian special days.

THE GARDEN OF EDEN

After God created man, He put him in a garden that He planted "eastward, in Eden" (Gen. 2:8 ASV) That there was such a place of perfection may be reflected in the Sumerian account of the land of Dilmun, which was pure, clean, and bright, where "the lion kills not, the wolf snatches not the lamb," where there was no disease or pain, deceit, or guile.[3]

Most discussion concerning the Garden of Eden has centered on its location. Scripture states that a river went out of Eden and parted into four separate rivers—the Pishon, Gihon, Hiddekel, and Euphrates (Gen. 2:11). The fourth is well known today. The third is an ancient name for Tigris. The first two have been identified by Professor Friedrich

[3]Pritchard, *Ancient Near Eastern Texts,* p. 38. The land of Dilmun was both a paradise and a real land. In the minds of many, Bahrain Island in the Persian Gulf has been connected with the land of Dilmun ever since Henry Rawlinson made the identification in 1861. A Danish expedition under the leadership of Geoffrey Bibby worked on the island for over fifteen years (beginning in 1953) and believed it to have been the seat of power in a fairly extensive empire. Actually, remains of a Dilmun civilization have also appeared far to the north in Kuwait and to the south in Abu Dhabi. Dilmun reached its zenith as a sea-trading power about 2000 B.C. See Geoffrey Bibby, *Looking for Dilmun* (New York: New American Library, 1969).

Delitzsch as the *Pisanu* and *Guhana*—two irrigation canals of Mesopotamia.[4] Such a view is fraught with problems, however, because for one thing, the irrigation culture of ancient Mesopotamia developed during the fourth and especially the third millennia B.C., long after the Flood. Irrigation canals would not have existed as early as the Garden of Eden.

The Gihon is related in Genesis to the "land of Cush," generally identified as Ethiopia; and Scripture seems clearly to put the origin of civilization in the Mesopotamian valley. The difficulty over the identification of Cush may be removed on the supposition that the Genesis 2:13 and 10:8 references to Cush apply to an Asiatic Cush. Cush initially may have been located in Arabia, from which Cushites could have spread to lower Mesopotamia and across the Red Sea into Africa. It is common knowledge that Semites periodically moved out of Syria or the Arabian peninsula into lower Mesopotamia. And at an early date some of them migrated to Ethiopia. The ruling house of Ethiopia claimed descent from Solomon and the Queen of Sheba (in Arabia) down through the days of the last emperor, Haile Selassie. Another difficulty in identifying the two lesser-known rivers that flowed from the area of Eden results from the fact that evidently the Noahic flood changed the geographical condition of Mesopotamia considerably.

Some have held that the Garden of Eden was located in Central Asia, and others have argued for the North Pole (which used to have a more temperate climate). Professor Delitzsch located Eden just north of Babylon, where the Tigris and Euphrates come close together. Others, impressed with Babylonian inscriptions, have located it just north of the Persian Gulf. Babylonian legend has it that in the neighborhood of Eridu (near the Gulf) was a garden, a holy place, in which there grew a sacred palm. Many inscriptions picture the palm with guardian spirits standing on either side. Possibly the view that the Garden of Eden

---

[4]G. F. Wright, "Eden," *International Standard Bible Encyclopedia*, 2nd ed., II, 898.

was planted in Armenia, where the Tigris and Euphrates originate near each other, is a plausible one. It is to be remembered that the river that parted into four rivers flowed out of Eden.

Probably we shall never be sure exactly where Eden was located. The effects of the Noahic flood on the topography of the Near East may have been devastating, making it impossible to determine geographical locations in earliest times on the basis of present conditions. The courses of rivers could have been greatly altered, and some rivers could have disappeared entirely. It does seem, however, that Near Eastern archaeology tallies with Scripture in demonstrating that the Mesopotamian area was the cradle of civilization. Albright says, "Archaeological research has thus established beyond doubt that there is no focus of civilization in the earth that can begin to compete in antiquity and activity with the basin of the Eastern Mediterranean and the region immediately to the east of it—Breasted's Fertile Crescent.[5] To be more specific, Braidwood, in discussing the development of civilization, says of Mesopotamia, "Things first happened there."[6] About all we can say with any degree of certainty at the present time is that Eden was probably located in or near ancient Mesopotamia (modern Iraq).

[5] William F. Albright, *From the Stone Age to Christianity,* 2nd ed. (Baltimore: Johns Hopkins Press, 1946), p. 6.

[6] Robert J. Braidwood, *Prehistoric Men,* 7th ed. (Glenview, Ill.: Scott Foresman, 1967), p. 136.

2 | THE FALL OF MAN AND EXTENSION OF CIVILIZATION

Genesis 3–5

THE FALL OF MAN

After Adam and Eve had enjoyed the pleasures of Eden for some time, Satan tempted them to sin. Their disobedience brought God's curse on themselves, their posterity, and on nature. In subsequent chapters of Genesis, the effects of sin are vividly portrayed in such events as the murder of Abel (Gen 4); in the "morgue" of chapter 5, where the phrase "and he died" constantly appears; and in the occasion for the Flood (Gen. 6). Throughout the rest of the Bible the pall of sin hangs heavy. Paul observed, in speaking of Adam, that "by one man sin entered into the world, and death by sin" (Rom. 5:12).

Because of the great impact of the Fall on all of society, we might expect to find extrabiblical indications of Adam's disobedience. Many have found such indications in the so-called "temptation seals" and the Adapa myth. In the last century a seal was found at Nineveh depicting a man and a woman seated on either side of a fruit tree; to the left of the woman "stands" a serpent.[1] In 1932, E. A. Speiser of the

---

[1] I. M. Price, O. R. Sellers, E. Leslie Carlson, *The Monuments and the Old Testament* (Philadelphia: Judson Press, 1958), p. 116.

University of Pennsylvania found a similar seal at Tepe Gawra in Mesopotamia portraying a man, a woman, and a serpent. These seals may preserve a tradition of the actual temptation in Eden. It should be noted, however, that at least on the seal from Nineveh the man and woman are fully clothed. Genesis describes Adam and Eve as naked before the Fall (Gen. 2:25).

While the "temptation seals" bear no inscription and leave us to guess at their meaning, the Adapa myth is a narrative of considerable length. The myth is preserved on four fragments, three from the famous library of Ashurbanipal at Nineveh and a fourth from the Amarna tablets in Egypt. How a copy of this myth found its way to Egypt is a matter of conjecture and need not detain us here.

Adapa was the principal character of the drama. As the story goes, Ea, patron god of Eridu, created Adapa and endowed him with great wisdom but not eternal life. Adapa was a semidivine person who served as priest of the temple of Ea in Eridu and had the special responsibility of providing bread and fish for the sanctuary. Once when Adapa was out fishing, the south wind capsized his boat, whereupon Adapa broke the wing of the south wind so it could not blow for a week. The great god Anu summoned Adapa to heaven to explain his action. Ea, fearful for the safety of Adapa, warned him not to accept the bread and water that would be offered him in heaven because it would be bread and water of death. This advice Adapa heeded. Upon his arrival in heaven, Adapa managed to obtain the good will of Anu, and the great sky god decided to offer him the bread and water of life. When Adapa refused to eat and drink, Anu declared, "Thou shalt not have eternal life! Ah, perverse mankind!"[2] And Adapa was returned to earth confirmed in his mortal state.

Actually there seems to be little connection between the Adapa myth and Genesis 3. It is true that the "food of life" is similar to the "tree of life" and that the principal character in

---

[2]James B. Pritchard, ed., *Ancient Near Eastern Texts Relating to the Old Testament,* 2nd ed. (Princeton: Princeton University Press, 1955), p. 102.

each narrative suffers death for failure to eat a certain kind of food. But the differences between the accounts are very great. Adam lost a chance at immortality because he succumbed to the temptation of the serpent and *disobeyed* God. Adapa forfeited immortality because he *obeyed* his creator. The exalted monotheism of the Genesis account far outshines the polytheism of the Mesopotamian legend. And, as Unger pointed out, a fall with its consequent punishment was impossible in Babylonian society, which was supposedly created by deities who were themselves evil.[3] It is difficult to say what connection, if any, exists between Genesis 3 and the Adapa myth. Perhaps the latter is merely an attempt to account for the mortality of man and for that reason it bears superficial similarity to the Genesis narrative. Or possibly the Adapa legend reflects a modicum of knowledge of the Fall still retained in the thinking and literature of the Babylonians.

BEGINNINGS OF CIVILIZATION

When man was created is not certainly known. Many have felt that by adding up the years of early men appearing in the genealogies of Genesis 5 and 11 and supplementing that information with chronological indications elsewhere in Scripture, it is possible to arrive at the dates for the creation of man and the beginning of civilization. It seems, however, that the genealogies of Scripture are designed primarily to provide representative names in the line of the Redeemer and that there are gaps in these genealogies. If such is the case, it is impossible to determine when the human race began. Moreover, archaeological excavations are constantly pushing back the dates of human history.[4]

Not only are we uncertain when man was created, we

[3] M. F. Unger, *Archaeology and the Old Testament* (Grand Rapids: Zondervan, 1954), p. 42.

[4] For a discussion of the question of gaps in biblical chronology, see Oswald T. Allis, *The Five Books of Moses* (Philadelphia: Presbyterian and Reformed, 1943), pp. 261–64; Gleason L. Archer, Jr., *A Survey of the Old Testament Introduction,* 2nd rev. ed. (Chicago: Moody Press, 1973), pp.

do not really know when to peg the dawn of civilization. But some light has been thrown on the latter question by discoveries in Mesopotamia and Palestine since World War II. At M'lefaat and Zawi Chemi in northern Iraq traces of rounded hut plans have been found. A carbon-14 date of about 8900 B.C. has been assigned to materials at Zawi Chemi (probably earlier than M'lefaat), where the people seem to have depended on direct supply from Mother Nature rather than producing their own food.

Since Cain was a "tiller of the ground" (Gen. 4:2) and not merely a food gatherer, it is necessary to look elsewhere for a development of culture relating to the biblical narrative. Robert Braidwood, professor of prehistory at the Oriental Institute of the University of Chicago, holds that Jarmo, just east of the modern oil town of Kirkuk, is the earliest known site of "the village-farming era." Braidwood reported a carbon-14 date of about 6750 B.C. for materials excavated at Jarmo. In three seasons there (1948–51) he did considerable work on the twenty-seven-foot depth of deposit, representing "approximately a dozen layers of architectural renovation and change." He observed that Jarmo inhabitants grew barley and two kinds of wheat, used flint sickles for harvesting their grain, had mortars with which to crack it, ovens in which to parch it, and stone bowls from which to eat it. They domesticated the goat. And bones of sheep, cattle, pigs, horses, and dogs appear in the occupational levels; it is not sure that they had domesticated these, however.[5]

During the years 1952 to 1958, Kathleen Kenyon and the British School of Archaeology in Jerusalem conducted excavations at Jericho. Much of Miss Kenyon's attention was concentrated on the preliterary levels of the site. On the

185–89; Merrill F. Unger, *Introductory Guide to the Old Testament* (Grand Rapids: Zondervan, 1951), pp. 192–94; and B. B. Warfield, *Studies in Theology* (New York: Oxford, 1932), pp. 235–58.

[5] Robert Braidwood, *Prehistoric Men,* 7th ed. (Glenview, Ill.: Scott Foresman, 1967), pp. 116–20.

basis of carbon-14 datings, she assigned a date of about 8000 B.C. to early village culture there.[6] The fact that carbon-14 dates for the beginnings of village life at Jericho may be earlier than those for Mesopotamia does not seriously challenge the claim that civilization began in the Tigris–Euphrates area. Even if one accepts these carbon-14 dates, which some question, the establishment of one very early village site in the Jordan Valley does not negate the fact that numerous very early towns sprang up in Mesopotamia with a civilization more advanced than anywhere else. Certainly the use of the wheel, writing, and other trappings of civilization appeared first in Mesopotamia.

There was no evidence of the use of metal by the villagers of Jarmo and early Jericho. But Genesis 4:22 states that near the dawn of civilization Tubal-cain was an instructor in the science of metallurgy and craftsmanship in bronze and iron. The use of copper became fairly common by 4000 B.C. or earlier, as evidenced by discoveries at such sites as Halaf and Chagar Bazar in northwest Mesopotamia and at several places in Anatolia. While not generally used at an early time, iron was known by around 2500 B.C. Henri Frankfort at Tell Asmar (ancient Eshnunna), northeast of Baghdad, discovered evidence of iron in a level which he assigned to 2700 B.C. (Probably this level would now be dated approximately 2500 B.C.) He found a bronze knife handle with the blade missing and small pieces of corroded metal rattling around in the handle. Sending these to a laboratory for analysis, he learned that the corroded blade had been iron.[7] Incidentally, it should be observed that the dates appearing in this paragraph do not establish a date for Tubal-cain.

In tying up these discoveries with the origins of civilization, one must take into account the destructive effects of the Flood. If the Flood was as destructive as Scripture seems to imply, it is possible that it wiped out all

---

[6] Kathleen Kenyon, *Archaeology in the Holy Land,* 3rd ed. (London: Ernest Benn, 1970), p. 331.

[7] Henri Frankfort, *Iraq Excavations of the Oriental Institute 1932/33,* pp. 59–62.

prediluvian traces of culture and that Jarmo and Jericho discoveries point to post-Noahic life. If so, the dates assigned to materials found by Braidwood and Kenyon do more to establish the date of the Flood than a date for the beginnings of civilization.

THE LONG-LIVED PATRIARCHS

Genesis 5 lists a number of men who lived for hundreds of years each. This passage has long been the subject of discussion, and efforts to explain the phenomenon have not been satisfactory. It is interesting to observe, however, that greater length of human life in the earliest periods of human history is also indicated in Babylonian literature. From the writings of Berossos, a Babylonian priest of the third century B.C., the existence of a Sumerian King List, which reported unbelievably long reigns of kings before the Flood, has long been known. In 1923 Stephen Langdon of Oxford published an almost complete text of the Sumerian original.

The original lists eight prediluvian kings ruling a total of 241,200 years at five Mesopotamian cities. The longest reign is 43,200 years and the shortest 18,600. Berossos spells the names quite differently, lists ten names instead of eight, and exaggerates the total to 432,000 years. Various efforts have been made to relate the biblical names to those of the other two lists, with dubious success.[8] It is interesting to speculate, however, that the Sumerian King List, though greatly exaggerated, may preserve a tradition of greater longevity before the Flood. Reigns assigned to kings after the Flood rapidly decrease until by the end of the list they are down to 100 years. This same decrease in longevity is to be observed in subsequent chapters of the Pentateuch.

---

[8] For discussion see George A. Barton, *Archaeology and the Bible*, 7th ed. (Philadelphia: American Sunday-School Union, 1937), pp. 317–26; and John Walton, "The Antediluvian Section of the Sumerian King List and Genesis 5," *Biblical Archaeologist* (Fall 1981), pp. 207–8.

3 | THE FLOOD

Genesis 6–10

FLOOD LAYERS

In 1929 the Christian public of the West was electrified by newspaper headlines screaming the discovery of evidence of the biblical flood. C. Leonard Woolley had found an eight-foot deposit of river mud in the middle of an early level of occupation at Ur. Clearly this was evidence that a flood had interrupted the occupation of the place early in the fourth millennium B.C., and Woolley was confident that he had found evidence of the Noahic flood.[1] Woolley commented, " . . . there could be no doubt that the flood of which we had thus found the only possible evidence was the Flood of Sumerian history and legend, the Flood on which is based the story of Noah."[2] Others followed him in his interpretation; and in subsequent years flood layers were uncovered in nearby Mesopotamian towns. Popular handbooks have come to assume that the flood layers from these towns constitute evidence for the occurrence of the biblical flood.

---

[1] C. L. Woolley, *Ur of the Chaldees* (Harmondsworth, Middlesex, England: Penguin Books, 1950), pp. 22, 23.
[2] Ibid., p. 23.

But what are the facts? At Ur, Woolley found flood layers in only two of the five shafts he dug down through the early strata there. So this flood of which he found traces did not even cover the whole city. Moreover, the flood deposit at Kish (near Babylon) dated well after 3000 B.C.— perhaps about 2800 B.C. The one at Fara (halfway between Ur and Babylon) dated well before 3000 B.C. And the one at Nineveh was a little earlier than the one at Ur—or possibly it should be dated about the same time as the one at Ur. Obviously these layers do not all point to the same flood. Furthermore, Woolley found no evidence of a flood at Obeid, four miles from Ur. Nor have other excavators found indications of a flood elsewhere in Mesopotamia. And no flood layers have been found in excavations in Syria, Palestine, and Egypt.[3] It seems clear, then, that river mud deposits found in some Mesopotamian mounds do not have any connection with the biblical flood. These deposits are not found everywhere and those found do not date to the same time.

One might conclude, as some have, that the biblical flood narrative was based on and was merely an exaggeration of one of the insignificant local floods mentioned above. But it appears that the Genesis flood at least engulfed all of mankind, if not the whole earth, because of clear indications in the Genesis narrative and because on all continents and among almost all peoples of the earth flood accounts have been found. These accounts all refer to a destructive flood occurring early in the respective tribal histories. In each case one or a few individuals were saved and were charged with repopulating the earth. To date, anthropologists have collected between 250 and 300 such flood stories.

THE SEARCH FOR THE ARK

When one launches a search for Noah's ark, he needs to know where to look. The Bible says the ark rested on "the

[3]John Bright, "Has Archaeology Found Evidence of the Flood?" *Biblical Archaeologist,* 5:4 (December 1942): 55–62; André Parrot, *The Flood and Noah's Ark* (New York: Philosophical Library, 1955), pp. 45– 53.

mountains of Ararat" (Gen. 8:4), not on "Mount Ararat," and thus raises the possibility that the ark could have landed on any one of several spots. The traditional site, Ağri Dağ, on the Russian border in eastern Turkey, is usually seized on because it is the highest mountain (16,946 feet) in the chain and in the entire Near East. But ancient traditions point to at least six other landing places, and some evangelical Christians and many others would leave the question of the location of Ararat open.[4] Most, however, would seem to favor the traditional site and might be even more dogmatic than Gleason Archer, who asserts a "good 70% probability that the modern Mt. Ararat is truly the one referred to in Genesis 8:4."[5]

If the traditional site is assumed, it must next be asked what, if anything, has been found there. A useful catalog of testimony concerning the existence of the ark and explorations of Ararat, beginning with the Babylonian historian Berossos in the third century B.C.., may be found in John W. Montgomery's *Quest for Noah's Ark*. This is the most scholarly book among the several popular paperbacks on the search for the ark; and part of it is a translation of Greek, Latin, and French sources. Montgomery himself climbed the mountain in 1970, 1971, and 1974.

The account of the discovery of the ark most widely publicized in American tracts, magazines, and newspapers during World War II concerned its purported sighting by Russian soldiers during World War I. According to the story, a Russian aviator serving on the Turkish front had sighted the ark in 1916. His report was transmitted to the Czar, who ordered a company of soldiers to engage in a surface exploration the following year. The Russian troops claimed to have seen a large ship or barge partly submerged in a swampy area on Mount Ararat. The records of this expedition disappeared in the ensuing Russian revolution, but some of the soldiers involved in it migrated to the

---

[4] Edwin Yamauchi, "Is That an Ark on Ararat?" *Eternity* (February 1978), pp. 27–32.

[5] Gleason Archer, "Is Ararat Known?" *Eternity* (February 1978), p. 29.

United States and spread the story here. Many efforts to trace the authenticity of the report came to naught, and there was a tendency to repudiate it altogether; but Montgomery claims authentication of the account.[6]

After World War II, when it was possible to launch expeditions to the Ararat region, interest in finding the ark drew many to this inhospitable mountain. In 1949, Dr. Aaron Smith, a retired missionary living in Greensboro, North Carolina, tried fruitlessly to find Noah's fabulous boat. His searches in the Ararat area, conducted in August and September, were eagerly followed by the press.[7]

Smith's failure did not stop efforts to find the ark. Three years later a French expedition headed by polar explorer Jean de Riquier again sought Noah's ark on the steep slopes of Mount Ararat, with no success except to plant the French tricolor atop the mountain. But an associate of de Riquier on this expedition, Fernand Navarra, is especially noteworthy because he climbed Ararat again in 1953, 1955, and 1969. In 1955 he produced a 5-foot beam of wood which he said came from a 35-foot deep crevasse at about the 13,500 foot level on the mountain and which he asserted had been part of the ark. The wood was subjected to a variety of tests, such as lignite formation and fossilization, and was determined to be oak, hand-tooled and partly fossilized, about 5,000 years old. Carbon-14 tests did not jibe with these conclusions, however, and indicated that the wood was only 1,500 years old or less.[8] In 1969 Navarra agreed to guide a SEARCH, Inc., team up the slopes of Ararat. Members of the team found several small pieces of wood identical to Navarra's wood under the ice near the supposed location of Navarra's 1955 find.

---

[6]John W. Montgomery, *The Quest for Noah's Ark* (Minneapolis: Bethany Fellowship, 1974), pp. 119–25.

[7]See the following references in *The New York Times* during 1949: April 13, p. 5; May 31, p. 18; July 2, p. 4; July 15, p. 12; July 27, p. 15; August 17, p. 16; August 22, p. 3; August 28, p. 14; August 29, p. 1; September 3, p. 16; September 10, p. 19; September 30, p. 25.

[8]Fernand Navarra, *Noah's Ark: I Touched It* (Plainfield, New Jersey: Logos, 1974), pp. x–xi, 123–37.

Professor Lloyd Bailey of Duke University has undertaken a scientific study of the dating of Navarra's wood samples. His conclusion is that the methods of dating, other than the carbon-14 method, used to date this wood are highly subjective and unreliable. This conviction was established on the basis of testimony of numerous scientists. In fact, one spokesman at North Carolina State thought that on the basis of lignitization, the 1955 specimen might date to the early centuries of the Christian era instead of 5,000 years ago. Bailey notes that carbon-14 analyses of the 1955 wood by three separate laboratories pegged the date in the eighth century A.D. and analyses of the 1969 wood by two laboratories put the date of that material in the seventh century A.D. A century of divergence can be explained if the samples come from two different oak logs. In any case, this wood apparently dates to the seventh or eighth century *s.c. A.D. and therefore has nothing to do with Noah's ark.[9]

One needs to be careful about more than the dating of the wood samples when dealing with the Navarra expedition. There have been assertions in the Turkish press and in various books published in the United States that the explorer perpetrated a hoax to gain fame and fortune. For instance, it is claimed that the wood discovered in 1955 did not come from Ararat at all, and there is an air of suspicion surrounding the 1969 discovery.[10]

In 1960 a Turkish army captain made a discovery that sparked new interest in locating Noah's ark. On an aerial photo of a mountain twenty miles south of the traditional Ararat he saw a boat-shaped form some five hundred feet long. An expedition of American scientists found the formation at a 7,000-foot altitude. The two-day survey of the site was insufficient to permit any conclusion.[11]

Numerous expeditions of "arkeologists" scrambled up Mount Ararat in the 1960s and early 1970s looking for

[9]Lloyd R. Bailey, "Wood From 'Mount Ararat': Noah's Ark?" *Biblical Archaeologist* (December 1977), pp. 137–46.

[10]Tim LaHaye and John Morris, *The Ark on Ararat* (Nashville: Nelson, 1976), pp. 133–34, 158–60.

[11]*Life* (September 5, 1960), pp. 112–14.

Noah's ark, without much in the way of tangible results. A cultic group from Palestine, Texas, claimed to have been on Mount Ararat in 1974 and to have seen the ark from a distance of 2,000 feet. The CIA demonstrated that the photo of the ark they showed had been crudely retouched, and some question that they ever ascended the mountain.[12]

Then in 1974 Ararat expeditions abruptly came to a halt. Kurds in the area had become quite rebellious, and bad relations between Turkey and the United States had developed over Turkish resumption of opium poppy growing and the Turkish Cyprus invasion. But ark fever was kept at high pitch during the 1970s by the production of the film *In Search of Noah's Ark* and the sale of the book by the same name written by Dave Balsiger and Charles E. Sellier.

In 1983 the Turkish government eased restrictions in the Ararat region, and permits were given to a score of groups from the United States, West Germany, France, Japan, and Turkey, not all in search of the ark. Best known of the personalities at Ararat in 1983 was former astronaut James Irwin who was associated with International Expeditions of Monroe, Louisiana, led by Marvin Steffins. Irwin flew an army observation Cessna around the mountain four times and later accompanied a group of twenty-two climbers in searching two passes high on the mountain. The expedition found nothing, and Irwin concluded, "It's easier to walk on the moon."[13] Steffins led another expedition to Ararat on August 20, 1984, and claimed to have found a boat-shaped formation on the southwest side of the mountain at the 5,200-foot level. He brought a large collection of samples of wood and soil from the site for analysis in the United States.[14] The verdict is not yet in on this claim. Several other American teams hiked up the famous mountain in 1984 or were making plans to do so in 1985.

---

[12]LaHaye and Morris, *The Ark on Ararat,* p. 215.

[13]"Rush to Climb Ararat Gives Town a Lift," *New York Times,* September 18, 1983.

[14]"Have Explorers Found Remains of Noah's Ark?" *Gannett Westchester Newspapers,* August 26, 1984, pp. C1–2.

THE FLOOD IN
MESOPOTAMIAN LITERATURE

In connection with the question of prediluvian longevity, a Sumerian King List has already been mentioned. Line 40 of column 1 of this text states that "the deluge overthrew the land." It is easy for the Bible student to take a superficial view of this account and to assume that reference here is to the biblical flood. But closer examination seems to demonstrate that this was a very local flood. Just before this flood the city-state of Shuruppak in central Babylonia had dominated the Babylonian political scene. After the flood, control passed to Kish (a few miles south of Babylon). It would appear, therefore, that the flood referred to occurred at Shuruppak and so seriously crippled the city as to send her into political eclipse. Excavations have revealed evidence of a destructive flood at Shuruppak dating between 3000 and 2800 B.C.[15] Possibly this is the one referred to in the King List.

As intimated earlier, the library of Ashurbanipal found at Nineveh serves as a veritable mine of texts, some relating to Old Testament study. In this collection George Smith of the British Museum staff found part of a Babylonian deluge story on which he reported at the December, 1872, meeting of the Society of Biblical Archaeology in London. The interest of both scholars and the general public was intense. Demands were heard all over England for reopening the Nineveh excavations in order to find the missing portion of the account. The *Daily Telegraph* agreed to finance the expedition in return for exclusive reporting rights. The following May, Smith arrived at Nineveh and found a fragment of the flood epic after only about a week of excavation. Numerous other tablets agreeing with or

---

[15]Jack Finegan, *Light From the Ancient Past,* 2nd ed. (Princeton: Princeton University Press, 1959), p. 24.

slightly divergent from the Ashurbanipal copy have been found in several Mesopotamian cities.[16] And an earlier Sumerian account turned up at the end of the nineteenth century.[17] Then in 1965 W. G. Lambert and A. R. Millard assembled a collection of Babylonian tablets and fragments from the British Museum holdings to form about two-thirds of the Atra-hasîs Epic, the flood account copied out in the reign of Ammi-saduqa (seventeenth century B.C.), great-great grandson of Hammurabi. It is both a creation and a flood narrative in which Atra-hasîs, king of Shuruppak, is the flood hero; and it constitutes another literary form of the Sumero-Babylonian account of the creation and early history of man.[18]

The Sumerian flood version was inscribed on a tablet found at Nippur. Badly mutilated, the copy was probably written about the time of Hammurabi (c. 1700 B.C.), although the story it narrates is undoubtedly much older. As the fragment begins, some of the gods lament the impending flood which the company of gods as a whole has already decided to send on mankind. The god Enki sought to devise a plan for saving at least one man—Ziusudra, the king and administrator of the temple provisions. Ziusudra was told to stand by a wall, where he was warned of the flood and apparently instructed to build a boat, though the text is missing at that point. Then a great rain swept over the land for seven days and nights. Afterward the sun came out and Ziusudra worshiped before the sun god and offered a sacrifice of an ox and several sheep. Subsequently the gods bestowed immortality on the hero of the flood story and

---

[16] For an account of these texts see Parrot, *The Flood and Noah's Ark,* pp. 32–34, 37–38, 41–42; Alexander Heidel, *The Gilgamesh Epic and Old Testament Parallels,* 2nd ed. (Chicago: University of Chicago Press, 1949), pp. 1–3.

[17] For information concerning this also, see Parrot and Heidel. The Sumerians were a non-Semitic people who occupied Mesopotamia by 4000 B.C. and dominated it during much of the fourth and third millennia.

[18] This is published as, W. G. Lambert and A. R. Millard, *Atra-Hasîs: The Babylonian Story of the Flood* (Oxford: Clarendon Press, 1969). See also Edmond Sollberger, *The Babylonian Legend of the Flood,* 3rd ed. (London: British Museum, 1971).

placed him in a paradise known as Dilmun, probably somewhere in the area of the Persian Gulf.

The Babylonian or Semitic flood story from Ashurbanipal's library is part of a longer work known as the *Gilgamesh Epic*. Written on twelve tablets, this epic tells about the search of Gilgamesh for immortality. In his search the hero[19] went to interview Utnapishtim, the Babylonian Noah who had gained immortality. Tablet 11 consists of Utnapishtim's description of the flood planned by the gods to destroy all mankind. The god Ea warned Utnapishtim of an impending flood on Shuruppak, his hometown. The god told him to prepare for it by tearing down his house and building a cube-shaped ship from the materials. This Utnapishtim did. The ship measured 120 cubits (about 65½ yards) on a side and had six decks. He caulked it with asphalt. Then he loaded the ship with his possessions, his family and relatives, craftsmen, cattle, and wild beasts. On the day appointed—when in the morning it rained bran and in the evening wheat, according to divine warning—Utnapishtim entered his ship and closed the door. All fury broke loose; even the gods in heaven were cowed with fear. Six days and nights the storm continued. On the seventh day the hurricane ceased and the hero opened the window and looked out on a scene of desolation. On Mount Nisir the ship came to rest. On the seventh day after that Utnapishtim sent out a dove which returned. Later he sent out a swallow which also failed to find a resting place. When a raven was sent out, it did not return. As the waters dried up, all the other animals and birds were released. Utnapishtim then offered a sacrifice. And when the gods smelled the odor they gathered like flies above the sacrificer. Then Enlil took the hero's hand and bestowed immortality and deity on both him and his wife.

As one compares the Genesis and Mesopotamian flood stories, he is impressed with the large number of similarities. Both accounts indicate that the flood was divinely planned, that it came as punishment for human failure or moral

---

[19] Gilgamesh was originally a historical personage who was a king at Uruk. The epic represents him as part god and part man—the son of the goddess Ninsun and an unknown mortal who was a priest at Uruk.

defection, and that the disaster was revealed to the flood hero. Both accounts assert that the hero was divinely instructed to build a boat which was pitched within and without, that a limited number of persons embarked in these ships with a considerable number of other living creatures to be saved alive, and that those not on board were destroyed. Both accounts also specify the physical causes of the flood, its duration, the landing place of the boat, and the sending out of birds. And in both accounts the heroes offer a sacrifice after the flood is over, receive a divine blessing, and are given some assurance that a similar catastrophe will never again overtake mankind.

The degree of similarity between the Genesis and Mesopotamian flood narratives has often been so emphasized that the extent of the differences between them has been obscured. Actually the differences are far greater than the similarities. Most significant among these differences is that the Babylonian and Assyrian stories are grossly polytheistic, while the Genesis narrative is characterized by an exalted monotheism. At every turn the Mesopotamian accounts exude polytheism. The Sumerian copy states that the assembly of the gods decreed the flood, but apparently not all gods of the pantheon concurred in the decision. Likewise, according to the Gilgamesh Epic the flood was decreed by "the great gods," but later some of them disclaimed responsibility for it and stigmatized one another for having brought on such a catastrophe. When the deluge began, the gods were "terror stricken," "fled," and "cowered like dogs and crouched in distress." After the deluge was over, the hero offered a sacrifice over which the hungry gods "gathered like flies."

Not only are the cuneiform accounts polytheistic, they are also pantheistic. The gods are identified with nature and the forces of nature they supposedly originated and over which they supposedly had control.

The reason for the flood is different in the two accounts. Genesis clearly indicates that God judged man with the deluge because of his sin. At the beginning of the Gilgamesh Epic the caprice of the gods seems to be responsible for the curse. Admittedly Ea's speech at the end of the Epic mentions man's sin as the cause of the flood but gives no details. The Atra-hasîs Epic states that Enlil sent the flood to destroy human beings because they were so noisy Enlil could not sleep.

In addition to these major differences, there are numerous lesser differences between the biblical and nonbiblical accounts.

1. *A period of grace.* Genesis 6:3 states that man was granted a 120-year reprieve from judgment, during which time he had ample opportunity to repent. On the other hand, the Mesopotamian deities jealously guarded their secret, giving man no opportunity for repentance. Even Ea found it necessary to use a dream to warn Utnapishtim of impending danger.

2. *Nature of the boat.* Figuring the biblical cubit according to the standard of 18 inches (more specifically, about 17.5 inches), Noah's ark was 450 feet long, 75 feet wide, and 45 feet high, with a displacement of about 43,300 tons. Supposing that the Babylonian cubit mentioned in the Gilgamesh Epic was the usual 20-inch measure (actually, the Mesopotamian "royal" cubit was about 19.8 inches long), Utnapishtim's ship was cubical, measuring 200 feet on a side, with a displacement of 228,500 tons. Moreover, the latter vessel had seven stories; Noah's had three.

3. *Occupants of the boat.* Utnapishtim took aboard his family and relatives, craftsmen, boatmen, gold and silver, and "beasts of the field," while Noah took only his wife, sons and their wives, and a specific number of living creatures according to the instructions of Genesis 6:19–21; 7:2–3.

4. *Physical causes of the flood.* The Gilgamesh Epic indicates that the flood was caused by cloudburst, mighty winds (probably of hurricane force), and the breaking of dikes and reservoirs. The Genesis account mentions heavy rains and implies that these were accompanied by some convulsion of the earth's crust, resulting in the release of subterranean waters (Gen. 7:11).

5. *Length of the flood (or rain).* The Sumerian narrative

says it rained for six days and nights; the Babylonian, seven days and nights. The Hebrew account declares it rained forty days and nights (Gen. 7:11).

6. *Landing of the boat.* Utnapishtim's ship landed on Mount Nisir, usually identified with a mountain east of the Tigris River and 400 miles north of the Persian Gulf, whereas Noah's ark landed in the Ararat Mountains, considerably farther north, either in eastern Turkey or in adjacent territory in Russia.

7. *The birds.* According to the cuneiform account, a dove was sent forth first, then a swallow, and finally a raven. Noah sent a raven first and a dove on three separate occasions.

8. *Effect of the flood.* The Genesis account gives no hint that any human beings or animals not on the ark survived the deluge; but of the cuneiform accounts, at least the Atrahasîs Epic indicates that all men did not perish.[20]

9. *Blessing on hero.* Utnapishtim was granted immortality after the flood was over; Noah was not.

Though differences between the Hebrew and cuneiform flood accounts have been noted, the remarkable similarities have not been eliminated. And scholars have long puzzled over the relationship between the accounts. As in the case of the creation narratives and other accounts alluded to in this book, there are three possibilities: the Babylonians borrowed from the Hebrews, the Hebrews borrowed from the Babylonians, and both descended from a common original. The first view has not been thought likely because Mesopotamian flood accounts antedate the Genesis record by perhaps a millennium. It should be noted, however, that the Hebrew account could have existed orally long before it was written. The most widely accepted view is that the Hebrews borrowed from the Babylonians and purified the account of polytheistic elements. Alexander Heidel of the University of Chicago has shown quite effectively that arguments to this effect are not decisive.[21] The view that both the Hebrew and

---

[20] Heidel, *The Gilgamesh Epic and Old Testament Parallels,* pp. 259–60.

[21] Ibid., pp. 261–67.

Babylonian accounts descended from a common original is quite appealing. After all, Genesis gives Mesopotamia as the original home of the Hebrews and the place where civilization first began and where it made a fresh start after the Flood. What would be more likely than that many accounts of an early tragedy of such magnitude would be preserved by peoples who lived in Mesopotamia or had migrated from there? Perhaps with Price, et al., we may conclude: "One ancient religion did not borrow these universal traditions from another, but each possessed primitively these traditions in their original form. The Genesis record is the purest, the least colored by extravagances, and the nearest to what we must conceive to have been the original form of these accounts."[22] In accepting such a conclusion, we do not rule out divine inspiration. As has been noted before, biblical writers did not always write without access to source materials. But God overruled and directed in the choice of such materials, guaranteeing accuracy of the finished product.

---

[22]I. M. Price, O. R. Sellers, and E. Leslie Carlson, *The Monuments of the Old Testament* (Philadelphia: Judson Press, 1958), p. 127.

4 | *THE CONFUSION OF TONGUES*
Genesis 11

The evolutionist holds that the languages of the earth originated by a process of development, as romance languages developed from Latin. Scripture declares, however, that at a specific time in history God broke into the affairs of men and in an act of judgment deliberately originated a number of languages.

A reverent and intelligent Bible student may well believe that both the biblical and evolutionary viewpoints concerning the origin of language are true. At Babel, God did establish parent languages of the earth; from those, currently known languages developed. No one can deny that new languages have come into being in historic times. Certainly Latin does not have a history as ancient as Egyptian, nor Spanish and French a history as ancient as Akkadian.

As a result of the destructive higher criticism of the last century, the view has become prevalent that the Bible is full of myth and folklore. The story of the Tower of Babel is classified as a myth—a story that must have been invented at some time in Hebrew history to account for the diversity of language. According to those who hold such a view, this myth developed in connection with the ziggurats or stage towers of Mesopotamia. These ziggurats, over thirty of which are known to exist, were composed of successively smaller stages or stories of sun dried or burnt brick, on top of which was constructed a temple. The ziggurat most commonly associated with the origin of the Hebrew myth is the one at Babylon, some 295 feet high and originally consisting of seven stages with a temple on the topmost level.[1] The view would be, then, that someone saw this ziggurat and composed a myth about the origin of language; finally this myth found its way into the Book of Genesis.

We must ask, however, whether the account in Genesis 11 can be accounted for so simply. In Genesis 9:1 God specifically told Noah and his sons, "Be fruitful, and multiply, and replenish [literally, *fill*] the earth." In direct disobedience, their descendants were concerned lest they be scattered over the earth and in pride sought to build a city and tower as a rallying point and to symbolize or memorialize *their* greatness. This God could not condone. Genesis does not say that they intended to enter heaven by means of this tower or that they intended to use it for worship purposes. The Hebrew simply calls it a *migdal* ("tower"), which could be used for defense or a number of other purposes, and there is no indication that the builders planned to erect a temple on it so that the structure could serve as a "link between earth and heaven" as the ziggurats did. Moreover, the Genesis narrative implies that such towers had not been built before and that this would therefore be something unique in the experience of man.

The ziggurats of Mesopotamia on the other hand were built for the express purpose of worshiping a local deity, not as an evidence of disobedience to him. Furthermore, the larger ziggurats came about as a result of slow development over a period of millennia. The earliest consisted only of a clay brick platform with a temple on it; a stage tower of several stages did not appear until the third millennium B.C.,[2] long after the diffusion of languages. So if we assign any

---

[1] André Parrot, *The Tower of Babel* (New York: Philosophical Library, 1956), pp. 22, 26–43.

[2] Ibid., pp, 41–45.

credence to the Genesis narrative at all, there can hardly be any connection between the Tower of Babel and the ziggurat—at Babylon or anywhere else. Moreover, we should take into account the fact that the early Sumerian inhabitants of Mesopotamia are thought to have come from the mountains to the east, and the ziggurats may merely have been an effort on the part of these people to construct a manmade mountain in the plains so they might be nearer to their gods. In their original homes they built high places in the mountains. Having moved to the plains, they were forced to build artificial mountains before they could establish their high places in them.

In 1876 George Smith of the British Museum published a mutilated Assyrian tablet which seems to reflect the account of Genesis 11. This tablet indicates that the hearts of some of the people were evil and that at night the gods destroyed the work the people did on the ziggurat during the day. The account also mentions divine confounding of speech and scattering of the people abroad.[3] Possibly we have here evidence of a tradition of the origin of languages in Mesopotamian literature—a tradition which harks back to an actual historical event. If so, then there is no good reason for denying that another form of that tradition appears in Genesis 11. More than that, we may reverently believe that Genesis 11 provides the purer form, preserved by God Himself.

---

[3] George Smith, *The Chaldean Accounts of Genesis,* 4th ed. (London: Low, Marston, Searle & Rivington, 1876), pp. 160ff.

Part II

THE PATRIARCHS

GENESIS 11:31–50:26

5 | ABRAHAM

Genesis 11:31–25:18

ABRAHAM'S IDENTITY

Who was Abraham? Scripture alludes to him as Abraham the Hebrew, Abraham the patriarch, the father of the faithful, and the progenitor of the Hebrews. Above all, the Bible describes him as a man of faith—one who was absolutely faithful to God and who believed His word implicitly. He accepted the divine call to leave his home and go to a land he did not know. He was willing to sacrifice his only son, believing that God who had so commanded could restore Isaac to life (Heb. 11:19). Certainly these dramatic acts of faith would not have been possible if Abraham had not believed God for all the little things day by day. God honored Abraham's great faith and justified him because of it. In Paul's treatises on righteousness and justification (Rom. 4:1–4; Gal. 3:6–29), he used Abraham's justification by faith as a pattern for believers in this age. Not only did God reward Abraham personally for his faith, but He also made with him a perpetual covenant of blessing, which was later confirmed to Isaac and Jacob and to David and his successors.

Genesis also speaks of Abraham's greatness in other

terms. It describes his defeat of the kings of the East, his rescue of Lot before the destruction of Sodom, and his great material possessions. It implies that he gave up much in leaving Ur for lands unknown, and it describes the abundant material rewards that God gave him in exchange.

Old Testament critics of the latter nineteenth and early twentieth centuries were very skeptical of the greatness of Abraham, his possessions, and his faith. Many liked to describe him as an ignorant Arab sheik living in a nomadic state. For such a one it meant nothing to move from Ur to Haran and then on to Palestine. It involved no sacrifice. He merely pulled up stakes and moved on to better grazing lands. However, as a result of excavations at Ur (1922–34) by Sir C. Leonard Woolley, it became clear that Abraham was a product of a brilliant and highly developed culture and that it must have meant a good deal for him to leave "by faith" for unknown lands. Moreover, the view that the whole patriarchal narrative was historically inaccurate has been dealt telling body blows by continuing discoveries in the Near East. So the biblical description of Abraham as a wealthy patriarch who was a product of an urban society has been rehabilitated.

More recently, however, the idea has been advanced that Abraham was not merely a powerful patriarch but a merchant prince. Cyrus Gordon set forth this view on the basis of his interpretation of certain materials discovered at Ras Shamra in Syria. It seems that the King of Ugarit (ancient name of Ras Shamra) complained to the Hittite king at Boghaz-koi (near modern Ankara, Turkey) about the activities at Ugarit of Hittite merchants from Ura (somewhere in Hittite territory) whence came many of the Hittite merchants. The Hittite king replied by ordering Ura merchants to carry on trade at Ugarit only in the summer, to leave Ugarit in the winter, and forbidding them to own real estate at Ugarit.

Gordon feels that the Hebrew patriarchs fit into the general context of merchant activity indicated by the Ugarit literature, and he notes several biblical references that indicate that the patriarchs were merchants. Joseph told his brethren that if they could prove their honest intentions, they would be permitted to trade in the land (Gen. 42:34). The Shechemites gave permission to Jacob's household to "dwell and trade" and "acquire real estate" in their territory (Gen. 34:10). So the Shechemites gave the Hebrew merchants rights denied by the Hittite king. In Genesis 23 Abraham was permitted to buy land from Ephron the Hittite for 400 shekels of silver—called "current money with the merchant" (v. 16). Probably the Hittite king did not control policies as far south as Hebron. Moreover, besides this reference, Genesis 13:2 and 24:35 mention that Abraham was rich in gold and silver.[1]

So Gordon concludes that "the patriarchal narratives, far from reflecting Bedouin life, are highly international in their milieu, in a setting where a world order enabled men to travel far and wide for business enterprise. . . . Abraham comes from beyond the Euphrates, plies his trade in Canaan, visits Egypt, deals with Hittites, makes treaties with Philistines, forms military alliances with Amorites, fights kinglets from as far off as Elam, marries the Egyptian Hagar, etc."[2] While the Bible student may not be prepared to accept the idea that Abraham was part of the merchant movement described in the literature of Ras Shamra, or that Abraham lived so late, he will at least agree that Gordon has portrayed Abraham to be much more than the Bedouin nomad scholars a generation ago thought him to be.

Taking a very different approach from that of Gordon, Albright came to a similar conclusion about Abraham. Albright preferred to place Abraham in the twentieth or nineteenth century B.C. instead of the middle of the second millennium, and therefore did not connect him with any Ugaritic developments as Gordon had. Albright pointed to the work of Nelson Glueck, Yohanan Aharoni, and Beno Rothenberg, who in the 1950s traced the twentieth–nineteenth century B.C. caravan routes through the Negev and desert of north-central Sinai. Albright noted the discovery of

[1] Cyrus Gordon, "Abraham and the Merchants of Ura," *Journal of Near Eastern Studies* (January 1958), pp. 28–30.

[2] Ibid., p. 30.

literally hundreds of sites along the old caravan route from Suez through the wilderness of north-central Sinai to Kadesh-barnea and Gerar. Thence the routes made their way to Hebron, Jerusalem, Bethel, Shechem, Damascus, Aleppo, and other Syrian cities, to Mesopotamia and Asia Minor. Other routes passed through sites along the edge of the desert in Transjordan and through the Jordan valley.

Then Albright noted that Abraham came from the great commercial city of Ur and lived in the important commercial center of Haran, which means "caravan city." He spent time on the main trade route in Damascus, Shechem, Bethel, Hebron, Beersheba, and Gerar, and especially between Kadesh and Shur while he was a "foreign resident" in Gerar. It is to be remembered that during the latter period (Gen. 20:1) Abraham had a very large entourage. For the battle recorded in Genesis 14 he had been able to field 318 armed "retainers," who with their families would have constituted a community of at least a thousand. Albright argued that Abraham could not have survived in this virtually rainless desert unless he had been engaged in the rather extensive and lucrative caravan trade between Palestine and Egypt. And Albright noted the specific indication of Genesis 13:3, which he translated: "And his caravan journeyed by stages from the south (Negeb) to Bethel." Egyptian texts speak of donkey caravans numbering 500, 600, and even 1,000 operating in the Sinai and the Sudan during the twentieth–nineteenth centuries B.C. So Albright pointed to the great wealth of Abraham, his extensive community, and his commercial activities. He argued that though Abraham was semi-nomadic, he was not merely a nomad wandering where he wished in search of pasture and water supply.[3]

Using different data from those of Gordon or Albright, David Noel Freedman of the University of Michigan views Abraham as a "warrior-chieftain" and a "merchant prince" who "belonged to urban culture and civilization." Moreover, he postulates that if Abraham could not read and write,

---

[3] William F. Albright, *Yahweh and the Gods of Canaan* (Garden City, New York: Doubleday, 1968), pp. 51, 62–73.

he probably made use of professional scribes available to the
leaders of society in his day to help keep records of business
transactions and to prepare communications. In such a way
information could have survived for later generations.[4]

THE TIME WHEN ABRAHAM LIVED

Biblical chronology before the time of David has not
been very firmly established. It is therefore difficult to decide
exactly when Abraham lived. If one accepts without question reckonings based on the Hebrew text, he can develop a
rather firm date for Abraham. The Septuagint, the Greek
translation of the Old Testament, differs somewhat from the
Hebrew, however. And archaeologists have found other
reasons for modifying biblical chronology of the second
millennium B.C.

Let us start with the Hebrew text. Of course it will be
necessary to work backward from firmly fixed dates.
Solomon probably began to reign in 970 B.C. It is stated in
1 Kings 6:1 that the Exodus took place 480 years before the
fourth year of Solomon's reign, or about 1446. Exodus
12:40–41 puts the entrance of the patriarchs into Egypt 430
years earlier—about 1876. From a study of Genesis 12:4;
21:5; 25:26; and 47:9 it is inferred that the patriarchs
sojourned in Canaan 215 years, entering about 2091.[5] Since
Abraham was seventy-five when he entered Canaan, his
birth would be pegged at 2166 B.C.

If one should follow the Septuagint, he would arrive at a
somewhat different conclusion for the date of Abraham. The

---

[4] David N. Freedman, "The Real Story of the Ebla Tablets," *Biblical
Archaeologist* (December 1978), p. 158. Wiseman likewise argues that
Abraham was not a nomad and that in Canaan he was a recognized
"prince" among the people of the land (Gen. 23:5, 6) but probably not a
merchant prince. See D. J. Wiseman, "Abraham Reassessed," *Essays on the
Patriarchal Narratives,* ed. A. R. Millard and D. J. Wiseman (Winona Lake,
Ind.: Eisenbrauns, 1983), pp. 141–53

[5] In these references it is clear that Abraham entered Canaan at 75.
Isaac was born to him at 100. Isaac was 60 at Jacob's birth. Jacob was 130
when he stood before Pharaoh. A total of 215 years elapsed, then, between
Abraham's entrance into Canaan and Jacob's entrance into Egypt.

Septuagint rendering of 1 Kings 6:1 puts the Exodus 440 years before the fourth year of Solomon's reign, or about 1406 B. C. According to the Septuagint rendering of Exodus 12:40, the 430 years include some 30 to 40 years of the patriarchal sojourn in Canaan, as well as the bondage in Egypt. If we add about 175 years for sojourn in Canaan to the 430 years of bondage in Egypt to the date 1406, we arrive at about 2010 as the date for Abraham's entrance into Canaan and about 2085 for his date of birth.

For various reasons, which cannot be discussed here,[6] many archaeologists and biblical scholars have felt that the date of the Exodus should be assigned to the thirteenth century, perhaps around 1275 or a little later. If the Septuagint rendering of Exodus 12:40, is accepted and added to a 1275 date for the Exodus, then Abraham's entrance into Canaan must be pegged at 1880 and his birth at 1955.

Cyrus Gordon, following his view that Abraham was a merchant prince whose activities fit into the context described by the Ugaritic texts, preferred to place Abraham around 1500 B.C. or later. It should be observed that Gordon's view is based, among other things, on the theory that Abraham belonged to a particular movement of merchant princes. This theory disregards many of the indications of biblical chronology. Even if we accept the idea that Abraham was a traveling merchant, we need not necessarily place him so late. Babylonian traders were active in Asia Minor as early as the days of Sargon I (c. 2300 B.C.), and that trade was still important well after 2000 B.C. Is it not entirely possible that Abraham, from southern Babylonia, was part of a mercantile movement earlier than that suggested by Gordon?

Research of Nelson Glueck in the Negev (the great plain of southern Palestine) has thrown more specific light on the time of Abraham than the speculations of Gordon. It is to be remembered that Abraham traveled through this area to and from Egypt and on other occasions during his sojourn in

---

[6]See Howard F. Vos, *An Introduction to Bible Archaeology*, rev. ed. (Chicago: Moody Press, 1983), pp. 55–60.

Canaan. Comments Glueck, "Either the Age of Abraham coincides with the Middle Bronze I period between the twenty-first and nineteenth centuries B.C. or the entire saga dealing with the Patriarch must be dismissed, so far as its historical value is concerned, from scientific consideration."[7] If Glueck is right, the chronological reckonings in the Hebrew text, upon which our English Bibles are based, are not far from wrong. Perhaps the suggestion of about 2000 B.C. for Abraham, as made in many popular Bible handbooks, is still valid. It is significant that a number of men who have excavated at biblical sites in the Near East feel that archaeological investigation—taken in conjunction with historical and chronological indications—requires an early second millennium B.C. date for Abraham. One of these excavators commented to the writer that archaeologically oriented Old Testament scholars are much more convinced of the early second millennium B.C. date of Abraham than philologically oriented Old Testament scholars. The present writer tends to follow the chronology of the Hebrew (Masoretic) text rather consistently.

As noted above, Albright placed the patriarchal period in Palestine during the twentieth and nineteenth centuries B.C., and many other scholars not of an evangelical bent are of the same conviction. Further discussion of the date of the patriarchs appears later in this chapter under the heading "Palestine in Abraham's Day."

ABRAHAM'S HOMETOWN

According to Genesis 11, Abraham was born in Ur of the Chaldees and spent his early life there, until after his marriage. Though once an important city, Ur gradually disappeared from history sometime after the days of Cyrus the Great (sixth century B.C.) as a result of the change in the course of the Euphrates River which left the area without an adequate water supply for irrigation. Even the site of the

---

[7] Nelson Glueck, *Rivers in the Desert* (Philadelphia: Jewish Publication Society, 1959), p. 68.

famous metropolis was unknown until 1854, when J. E.
Taylor excavated briefly at Tell Muqayyar, 150 miles
northwest of the Persian Gulf, and identified it as Ur. In
1918 R. Campbell Thompson began further work there
under the auspices of the British Museum, followed later in
the same year by an expedition led by H. R. Hall, representing the same institution. The main work at the site,
however, was done by a joint expedition of the University
Museum of Philadelphia and the British Museum in a
protracted excavation headed by Sir C. Leonard Woolley
(1922–34).

Since discoveries at Ur revealed more than one period
of occupation, it becomes necessary to determine the one
with which Abraham should be associated. If one follows
the Hebrew text (see discussion above) he would conclude
that Abraham left Ur before her golden age (2070–1960 B.C.,
according to the minimal chronology). The Septuagint
chronology would demand that the date Abraham left Ur be
placed during her golden age.

Long before the days of Abraham, Ur boasted a high
development of civilization. Among the most remarkable
discoveries made there by Woolley were the royal tombs,
now dated by many scholars at about 2500 B.C. Since these
ancient people had a strong belief in the afterlife, royalty was
provided with all that might make such existence more
pleasant. Musical instruments, jewelry, clothing, utensils of
various kinds, wagons and beasts of burden, weapons, and
even servants were placed in the tombs. King A-bar-gi's
grave included sixty-five persons besides himself; Queen
Puabi's (formerly rendered Shubad's) contained twenty-
five.[8] In the absence of evidence of violent death, it is
supposed that these servants were either poisoned or
drugged and buried alive.

It is impossible here to describe all the tombs excavated
or the richness of the contents. The gold vases of Queen
Puabi, the gold helmet of Meskalam-dug, the elaborate

---

[8] Woolley, *Ur of the Chaldees,* p. 45.

headdresses of valuable metals and precious stones, the copper weapons and utensils all bespeak a high point of development in the civilization of Ur long before the days of Abraham. Woolley comments, "The contents of the tombs illustrate a very highly developed state of society of an urban type, a society in which the architect was familiar with all the basic principles of construction known to us to-day. The artist, capable at times of a most vivid realism, followed for the most part standards and conventions whose excellence had been approved by many generations working before him; the craftsman in metal possessed a knowledge of metallurgy and a technical skill which few people ever rivaled; the merchant carried on a far-flung trade and recorded his transactions in writing; the army was well organised and victorious, agriculture prospered, and great wealth gave scope to luxury . . . and as has been demonstrated . . . this civilisation was already many centuries old."[9]

It is possible that the Hebrew chronology is not exactly right and that Abraham knew Ur during her golden age (her third dynasty). The question of which period of Ur's history Abraham knew is further complicated by the dates one assigns to Mesopotamian developments. As noted, the writer has tended to follow the Hebrew biblical chronology and the minimal chronology of Albright for Ur III (2070–1960 B.C.), in which case Abraham would have left Ur before the golden age. But other chronologies for Ur III vary by several decades. For example, Carl Roebuck[10] dates the period 2135–2027; if one followed this chronology and the Hebrew chronology, he would envision Abraham as leaving at the beginning of the golden age. McGuire Gibson pushes the Ur III period back to 2200;[11] acceptance of his dating would result in putting Abraham's departure from Ur during the golden age.

[9] Ibid., pp. 67–68.

[10] Carl Roebuck, *The World of Ancient Times* (New York: Scribner's, 1966), p. 33.

[11] McGuire Gibson, *The Oriental Institute 1981–82 Annual Report*, p. 41.

Many have concluded that Abraham left for Haran
during Ur's golden age. Then Ur-Nammu was the guiding
light to prosperity. Under him the city with its far-flung
suburbs grew to be a flourishing metropolis of some
360,000.[12] Her commercial influence was felt as far north as
the Anatolian mountains, whence copper was secured, and
for a great distance south along the Persian Gulf, where
merchants obtained copper, gold, ivory, hardwoods, and
various types of stone. Within the city, factories produced
textile and metal goods for export, as well as for home
consumption. Fortunately for us, citizens of Ur made
elaborate records of all their transactions. Bills of lading,
invoices, letters of credit, court cases, tax records, and
practice tablets of the school boy all came to light when the
fingers of the excavator raised the curtain of time from the
mound of Muqayyar.[13]

Building operations were tremendous during this period, too. Ur-Nammu constructed around the city proper a
wall some two and one-half miles in circumference and 77
feet thick. Within this, in the northwestern part, was the
sacred, or Temenos, enclosure of the moon-god Nannar;
this measured about 400 yards long and 200 yards wide.[14]
Inside this enclosure stood the great brick ziggurat or stage-
tower of Nannar, measuring about 200 feet in length, 150
feet in width, and 70 feet in height. Each of the three stages
of the tower was smaller than the one below, and on the
topmost level stood the temple of the god. Gardens were
planted on the terraces. As was true of the Parthenon of
Greece many centuries later, the ziggurat at Ur was without
straight lines. By using ingeniously curved surfaces, the
architects were able to create an appearance of elegance and
grace not obtainable with straight lines.[15]

Education was also at a high stage of development in the

---

[12] C. L. Woolley, *History of Mankind*, vol. 1 (New York: New
American Library, 1965), 2:123–25

[13] C. L. Woolley, *Abraham* (New York: Scribner's, 1936), pp. 118–
33.

[14] Ibid., p. 79.

[15] Woolley, *Ur of the Chaldees,* pp. 92–96.

twentieth century B.C. The three R's were basic, but the great advancement in mathematics is a particular surprise. Besides the multiplication and division tables, the student was able to extract square and cube roots and do exercises in practical geometry.[16]

As to the dwellings of the period, Woolley observed that they might measure about forty feet in width and fifty in depth and consist of two stories, the first for household tasks, storage, and servant quarters, and the second for the family. The dwellings ranged in size from ten to twenty rooms, which were arranged around a central court open to the sky. With surprising modernity, the guest room was even adjoined by a lavatory.[17]

Whether Abraham left Ur before, during, or after her golden age, the city was great and offered much to her inhabitants. Although prosperity may have been sagging and Terah and the rest of the family may have had misgivings about the future, from the human standpoint it probably would have been easier to remain at Ur than to go somewhere else and start over again. It may mean little to twentieth-century American "men on the go" to pull up stakes and move several hundred miles away, but we have no right to project current ideas of mobility into the past. Moreover, while a modern American may think nothing of moving several hundred miles to a specific destination, he will require great faith to load his family and possessions in his car and start out on the road, not knowing where he is going. That was Abraham's experience. Furthermore, Abraham had to move through hostile, unpoliced territory; the modern American's road is policed all the way.

Though one may argue that Abraham left Ur during a time of political confusion, it is the opinion of the writer that such a view would not destroy the element of faith in Abraham's movements. After all, if he left merely because of political instability at Ur, where in the world could he expect to find security? Egypt is the only suggestion that can be

---

[16] Woolley, *Abraham,* p. 103.
[17] Ibid., pp. 111–15.

made, and there is no indication he intended to go there. Besides, if Abraham left Ur at the time indicated by the Hebrew chronology, he would have found Egyptian political power at a low ebb. (Egypt was in a period of political disintegration between the Old and Middle Kingdoms.) If he had gone to Egypt during the eighteenth century, he would have arrived in time to watch the Hyksos conquer the land of the Pharaohs. Regardless of when Abraham left Ur, he turned his back on a great metropolis, setting out by faith for a land about which he knew little or nothing and which could probably offer him little from a standpoint of material benefits.

Cyrus Gordon in his portrayal of Abraham as a merchant prince questioned the identification of the southern Babylonian Ur as the home of Abraham. Something has already been said about his view that Abraham was a merchant prince. In that discussion he mentioned an Ura alluded to in the Ras Shamra literature. That Ura (equivalent of Hebrew *Ur*) was located in northern Mesopotamia, probably northeast of Haran. Moreover, Gordon observes that Xenophon described the Chaldeans as a warlike people blocking the way to Armenia and as neighbors of the Armenians but at war with them, thus locating Chaldea in northern Mesopotamia.[18] It should be added that Gordon recognized the existence of the southern Ur of the Chaldees but claimed it was not the home of Abraham. Gordon's view has found little scholarly acceptance and H. F. W. Saggs has effectively answered it.[19]

CAMELS IN EGYPT

According to Genesis 12:16 Abraham had camels in Egypt. About two centuries later Joseph was taken to Egypt by a camel caravan (Gen. 37:25). At the time of the Exodus camels were among the animals affected by the murrain of cattle (Exod. 9:6). Camels are mentioned frequently in

---

[18]Gordon, "Abraham and the Merchants of Ura," p. 30.

[19]H. F. W. Saggs, "Ur of the Chaldees, a Problem of Identification," *Iraq* 22 (1960): 200–209.

subsequent passages of Scripture, but it is with these earlier references that we are concerned at this moment because they locate the camel in Egypt long before scholars have been prepared to admit the presence of camels there.

T. Eric Peet provided a good example of the common higher critical attitude when he said that "the camel was not introduced into Egypt until centuries after this period [time of Abraham]."[20] R. H. Pfeiffer classified the Genesis 12 reference as an obvious error.[21] A. H. Sayce put the introduction of camels into Egypt at the time of the Arab conquest (seventh century A.D.),[22] and the great Egyptologist A. Erman dated their appearance in Egypt to the Greek period.[23]

With the general rehabilitation of the historical and social accuracy of the patriarchal narrative in recent years has come also new information on the early appearance of the camel in Egypt. For the marshaling of this evidence we are particularly indebted to Joseph P. Free.[24] While admitting that the camel did not come into general use in Egypt until Greek and Roman times, Free found considerable evidence for the knowledge and use of camels in Egypt long before Abraham—whenever he might be dated. For instance, about 1935 a skull of a camel was found in the Fayum of Egypt (an oasis area southwest of Cairo), dating 2000–1400 B.C. Miss Caton-Thompson found a camel's hair rope in the Fayum during the 1927–28 season of excavation and dated it to the Old Kingdom (c. 2500 B.C.). Three pottery camel heads dating to about 3000 B.C. have also been excavated in Egypt. These are only a few of the evidences of the early use of the camel in Egypt that Free presented. In all, he described the

[20] T. Eric Peet, *Egypt and the Old Testament* (Liverpool: University of Liverpool Press, 1924), p. 60.

[21] R. H. Pfeiffer, *Introduction to the Old Testament,* rev. ed. (New York: Harper, 1948), p. 154.

[22] A. H. Sayce, *Patriarchal Palestine* (London: S.P.C.K., 1895), p. 171.

[23] A. Erman, *Life in Ancient Egypt* (London: Macmillan, 1894), p. 493.

[24] Joseph P. Free, "Abraham's Camels," *Journal of Near Eastern Studies* (July 1944), pp. 187–93

following evidence from the pre-Christian era: one item from the seventh century, one from the ninth, two from the thirteenth, one from the fifteenth, one from the sixteenth, two from the period between the fifteenth and twentieth centuries, one from the twenty-third, several from the twenty-fifth, four from the first dynasty (c. 3000 B.C.), and four from the predynastic period.[25] In recent years numerous indications of the domestication and use of the camel in Mesopotamia and Syria during the patriarchal period have come to light. K. A. Kitchen has collected some of this information.[26] So archaeological investigation has provided abundant objective evidence to confirm another assertion of Scripture that has been commonly assailed by the critics.

AN ALTAR AT MAMRE

Probably not more than five years after Abraham and Lot returned to Canaan from Egypt (Gen. 13:1), their herdsmen tangled over pasture and water rights. Flocks and herds had greatly multiplied, and supplies proved to be insufficient; so Abraham decided he and Lot should part. Given first choice, Lot took the fertile plain of the Jordan, which had not yet been ruined by the cataclysm that destroyed Sodom and Gomorrah (Gen. 13:2–12). Soon Abraham settled by the oaks of Mamre near Hebron and built an altar there (Gen. 13:18), and at the site he subsequently interceded with the heavenly messengers for the towns of Sodom and Gomorrah (Gen. 18:20–33).

The traditional site of Mamre is Ramat el-Khalil, about two miles north of Hebron. It is surrounded by a beautifully built wall enclosing an area measuring 150 by 200 feet. The wall was originally constructed by Herod the Great to enclose Abraham's altar and well, but it was partially wrecked during the warfare that destroyed Jerusalem and the Temple in A.D. 70. Hadrian rebuilt the wall in 130 and

[25] Ibid., p. 193.
[26] K. A. Kitchen, *Ancient Orient and Old Testament* (Chicago: InterVarsity Press, 1966), pp. 79–80; K. A. Kitchen, "Camel," *Illustrated Bible Dictionary* (Downers Grove, Ill.: InterVarsity Press, 1980), 1:228–30.

erected a pagan altar on the spot where Abraham's altar supposedly had been. When Constantine's mother-in-law Eutropia visited the site early in the fourth century and found the pagan altar still defiling the place, she informed the emperor. Constantine then ordered demolition of the altar and erection of a church within the enclosure. The church was torn down by the Persians in A.D. 614 and later partially rebuilt. After the Muslim conquest it fell into ruins.

Father A. E. Mader excavated the enclosure for the Görres-Gesellschaft (1926–28) and established its connection with Mamre and the Constantinian church. The church measured 66 by 54 feet. He also found remains of the Maccabean period and the Judean kingdom period, the earliest building remains dating to the ninth-eighth centuries B.C. But some materials dating to the Middle Bronze Age were discovered. Although tradition has connected this spot with Abraham for some 3,000 years, it cannot be demonstrated conclusively that this was indeed the place where he lived in tents about a millennium earlier.[27]

WAR WITH KINGS FROM THE EAST

Not long after Abraham settled at Mamre, four Eastern kings invaded the fertile valley, worsted the local rulers in battle, and made off with immense booty and numerous captives. Lot was listed among those carried away. Then Uncle Abraham rushed to the rescue.

It is clear from Genesis 14:4 that these kings of Southern Palestine had been tributary to Mesopotamian overlords for twelve years and thereafter had rebelled against what was probably extortionate rule. Within a year a punitive expedition was on the way. Chedorlaomer of Elam (in the area of modern west central Iran) led the pack. The invaders apparently resubjugated the entire Transjordan area as far south as Edom and Sinai and then circled north to deal with the rebellious towns at the southern end of the Dead Sea

---

[27] Avraham Negev, ed., *Archaeological Encyclopedia of the Holy Land* (London: Weidenfeld and Nicolson, 1972), p. 266.

(concerning location, see later discussion on destruction of Sodom and Gomorrah). The cities of the plain did not submit meekly. The kings of Sodom, Gomorrah, Admah, Zeboiim, and Zoar joined battle with the invaders in the Vale of Siddim. But they were no match for the superior Mesopotamian forces. Many fell in the bitumen pits which dotted the area; others escaped to the mountains. The enemy thoroughly plundered the unattended towns and carried off such captives as they were able to take, including Lot.

A refugee quickly ran to Abraham, who was near Hebron, and informed him of the devastating defeat. Immediately the patriarch armed his trained men and dashed off in pursuit. Abraham caught up with the kings of the East, defeated them and pursued them to Hobah, near Damascus. He then retrieved the booty and captives and returned to Sodom. The forlorn king and his remaining subjects gratefully offered the returning heroes all the plunder if they would only surrender the captives. For his part, Abraham refused any reward but acknowledged the right of his confederates to their share of the plunder. Apparently Lot and his family settled down in Sodom once more, and the cities of the plain began an uphill climb to regain their prosperity. No doubt they were quite successful in their efforts and the scars of war quickly healed. Genesis 18 and 19 give the impression of thriving prosperity and sizable population in the area. Nothing further is heard of the invaders. Perhaps changing fortunes in Mesopotamia prevented continuing warfare. Perhaps devastation of Transjordan was sufficient to prevent rebellion in that area extensive enough to call forth new military intervention. Within a few years the cities of the plain were to meet their doom, so the last possibility of rebellion in that quarter would be wiped out.

Historicity of the account. The historicity of Genesis 14 has often been questioned in the past, but there is now satisfactory circumstantial support, if not direct evidence, for the biblical account.

For a long time the names of the four kings of the East were thought to be unhistorical, but most scholars now find some means of identifying them with known persons or at least identifying them as historical name forms. Amraphel of Shinar frequently has been identified with Hammurabi of Sumer or Babylon. Shinar is a common designation for Babylonia, and Amraphel was thought to be the Hebrew rendering of Hammurabi. In the last couple of decades this identification seldom has been held because the date of Hammurabi has been pulled down to about 1700 B.C.— separating him from the time of Abraham—and because the identification is now commonly thought to be etymologically untenable. Albright has suggested the equation of Amraphel with Amud-pi-el ("Enduring is the word of El"), a king named in the Mari tablets and powerful in Babylonia in the century before Hammurabi.[28] While reference to Chedorlaomer has not yet been found in the inscriptions, it is often pointed out that there are two Elamite elements in his name: *Chedor (Kudur)*, found in various Elamite names; and *laomer*, the softening of the name of an Elamite goddess, Lagamar. Tidal, king of Goiim, has been identified with Tudhalias (several Hittite kings were so named); and Arioch, king of Ellasar, has been identified with Arriwuk (a name appearing in the Mari texts). Whether or not these identifications are accepted, it can readily be seen that Genesis 14 does not introduce fictional forms but good Near Eastern names. It may also be interesting to observe, in passing, that Babylonian clay tablets dating to the patriarchal period mention Abarama and Abamrama, very close in form to the Hebrew Abraham and often equated with Abraham, though of course they do not refer to the patriarch himself.[29]

Another reason why the historicity of Genesis 14 used to be questioned was the use of the unusual line of march through Gilead and Moab by the Eastern kings. Albright once "considered this extraordinary line march as being the best proof of the essentially legendary character of the narrative."[30] But in 1929 Albright himself discovered a line

---

[28] D. J. Wiseman, "Hammurabi," *Zondervan Pictorial Encyclopedia of the Bible*, III, 26.

[29] Jack Finegan, *Light From the Ancient Past*, p. 73.

[30] W. F. Albright, *Archaeology of Palestine and the Bible* (Cambridge, Mass: American Schools of Oriental Research, 1974), p. 142.

of buried cities running along the eastern edge of Gilead, between the desert and the forests of Gilead. Some of these mounds were of considerable size. Upon investigation, Albright found them to date to the Early Bronze (3000–2000 B.C.) and Middle Bronze (2000–1500 B.C.) ages.[31] The accuracy of Genesis 14 becomes more significant, and the evidence for early authorship of the account becomes more evident when we realize that this "Highway of the King" was probably never employed by invading armies after 1200 B.C.[32]

Third, the assertion made formerly that travel was not so extensive in the patriarchal period as indicated in this chapter and that military control of Palestine by Mesopotamian kings did not exist at that time must now be discarded. The expedition of kings of Elam and Babylonia appears in different light when we learn, for instance, that as early as 2300 B.C. Sargon of Akkad (near Babylon) made raids on the Amorites of Syria and Palestine. Of particular significance for the present study is the fact that prior to Hammurabi's rule in Babylon, Kudur-Mabug, an Elamite king of Larsa (north of Ur), claimed to be "prince of the land of Amurru," which may have included Palestine and Syria.[33] Furthermore, a wagon contract found at Mari in the Middle Euphrates region and dating to the patriarchal period gives as one of the conditions of rental that the wagon shall not be driven to the Mediterranean coastlands, hundreds of miles away.[34] This prohibition implies extensive travel during the period under consideration. Prohibitions are rarely stipulated unless the forbidden act has some likelihood of occurring.

Fourth, critics have questioned the ability of Abraham to defeat the hosts of the East with 318 servants (*hanîkîm,* an Egyptian word for armed retainers of Palestinian chieftains). An analysis of the biblical account readily provides an

---

[31] Ibid.

[32] Ibid.

[33] A. T. Clay, *Light on the Old Testament From Babel,* 2nd ed. (Philadelphia: Sunday School Times, 1907), p. 137.

[34] Joseph P. Free, *Archaeology and Bible History* (Wheaton, Ill.: Scripture Press, 1950), p. 57.

explanation. No doubt Abraham's attack was a rearguard action. It was the common practice of ancient armies for booty and captives to be placed in the rear while the main army marched ahead. It would be comparatively easy to overpower the rear guards and make off with the spoil. Second, this was a surprise attack at night. Under cover of darkness the attacked might well overestimate the strength of their attackers—especially if Abraham divided his force into many small companies, each with a torch (14:15). The number of companies of soldiers could have thrown the hosts of the East into complete confusion, as was true of those whom Gideon attacked many centuries later (Judg. 7:16–25). Perhaps the armies of the East had pitched camp. If so, they could easily have been routed by a small force in a surprise attack by night. Third, it should be remembered that biblical history constantly throws into the limelight the activities of important personages in the Hebrew–Christian tradition, when actually their part in a given event may have been much less in proportion than the Bible indicates. On this occasion Aner, Eschol, and Mamre and their retainers were confederate with Abraham (Gen. 14:13, 24). A complete narrative of the Abrahamic expedition might reveal that more than 1,000 men were involved in the combined armies and that Abraham was merely the moving spirit behind this expedition to which he contributed heavily.

As we continue to investigate the historicity of Genesis 14, we might well ask if any of the towns mentioned in verses 5 through 7 have yet been identified. At least three have been. Albright and Steuernagel have suggested that a modern place in eastern Gilead by the name of Ham is to be identified as the site of the ancient town of the same name. Albright discovered a mound nearby containing ruins dating back to the Bronze Age (which ended in 1200 B.C.).[35] Nelson Glueck identified Ashteroth Karnaim, probably a composite of two names, with two sites close together in southern Syria: Tell Ashtarah and Sheikh Sa'ad. The latter was called

[35] Albright, *Archaeology of Palestine and the Bible*, p. 142.

Carnaim during the early Christian Era. En-mishpat, or Kadesh Barnea, he identified with Ain el-Qudeirat in the Sinai Peninsula.[36] Ain el-Qudeirat is now generally identified with Kadesh-Barnea. The site was first explored by C. L. Woolley and T. E. Lawrence in 1914. They found a Judean fortress there, built to protect the southern border of Judah. Moshe Dothan worked there in 1956 and Rudolf Cohen in 1976 to 1979. Three superimposed fortresses of the tenth to sixth centuries have been identified. To date nothing has been found at the site dating to the patriarchal age, but there is a concentration of Middle Bronze 1 (2200–2000 B.C.) settlements throughout the region.[37]

It has already been observed that the kings of the East moved very far south and then swung north to deal with Sodom and Gomorrah. Possibly it was the valuable mineral deposits of the area that led them as far south as Kadesh Barnea. There were important deposits of copper, manganese, and other minerals in Seir and Midian. The ancient copper mines of Seir (Edom) were studied a few years before World War II, and the ancient copper and gold deposits of Midian and the copper of Sinai have been known since the turn of the century. Manganese appears in large quantities southeast of Edom.[38] One should be very cautious about suggesting the lure of metals as the magnet that drew the invading force so far south. The work of Beno Rothenberg in the Timna Valley (some fifteen miles north of the Gulf of Aqaba) from 1964 to 1970 showed that while copper smelting in the area was known in the fourth millennium B.C., it did not occur again until the fourteenth to the twelfth centuries B.C.[39] Albright thought that the campaign was directed against the Egyptians.[40]

Certainly all of the discussion just entered into abun-

---

[36] Glueck, *Rivers in the Desert,* p. 73.

[37] Rudolph Cohen, "Excavations at Kadesh-barnea 1976–1978," *Biblical Archaeologist* (Spring 1981), pp. 93–107.

[38] Albright, *Archaeology of Palestine and the Bible,* pp. 143, 211–12.

[39] Beno Rothenberg, *Were These King Solomon's Mines?* (New York: Stein and Day, 1972).

[40] Albright, *Yahweh and the Gods of Canaan,* p. 69.

dantly confirms the historicity of the once-doubted account of Genesis 14. Another good example has been given of how archaeology confirms the accuracy of the Bible, or at least general validity or plausibility in cases when some specifics cannot be checked. In conclusion, it may be useful to quote one who often capitulated before higher critical assertions: ". . . there seems no reason to question a factual basis of Genesis 14."[41]

Having demonstrated the accuracy or plausibility of this account, we might next ask when the events occurred. Something has already been said about the time when Abraham lived, but perhaps a further word on dating is in order here. Albright prefers to date it towards the end of the nineteenth or the beginning of the eighteenth century B.C.[42] Unger follows the Masoretic chronology rather rigidly and therefore holds to a period around the middle of the twenty-first century B.C.[43] Nelson Glueck bases his dating on his explorations along the line of march of the Eastern kings. He found that every village in the path of these Eastern kings was plundered and destroyed, the countryside laid waste, and for hundreds of years thereafter left uninhabited, its monuments broken and strewn on the ground. This great destruction he dates to the nineteenth century B.C.[44] While the pottery chronology of the areas investigated by Glueck may need further refinement, resulting in some adjustment of his dates, his conclusions are probably not very far from the truth.

ABRAHAM AND THE PROBLEM OF AN HEIR

After Abraham had put things back on even keel at Sodom, he began to take stock of his personal affairs. Well over age seventy-five, he was still childless. And he complained to God that his heir was a servant by the name of

---

[41] Caiger, Stephen L. *Bible and Spade* (London: Oxford University Press, 1951), p. 34.

[42] Albright, *Yahweh and the Gods of Canaan*, p. 69.

[43] M. F. Unger, *Archaeology and the Old Testament*, p. 118.

[44] Glueck, *Rivers in the Desert*, pp. 73–74.

Eliezer (Gen. 15:2–3). To a modern Occidental mind such an idea seems strange. But the Nuzu tablets, coming from central Mesopotamia and dating about 1500 B.C.,[45] demonstrate that it was common practice for a person's slave to become his heir. At Nuzu childless people did on occasion adopt slaves or free men. The adopted son then assumed the responsibility of caring for his foster parents in advanced age and burying them and mourning for them. In return the adopted son became heir. If, however, the adopter later begat a son, the real son became the chief heir.[46] But God told Abraham that he would have a son by natural procreation (Gen. 15:2–4).

When Abraham turned eighty-five, he was still childless. Sarai (later called Sarah) was barren. So, according to the custom of the time, she gave a handmaid named Hagar to Abraham as a concubine. Then, when Hagar was with child, she began to despise her mistress. "And Sarai treated her harshly, and she fled from her presence" (Gen. 16:6 NASB). Again it seems strange to us for the patriarch to be conducting himself in such fashion. But a study of Scripture and supporting information from archaeology indicates that the main purpose of marriage in patriarchal times was procreation. Both the Code of Hammurabi and Nuzu tablets permit a man to take a concubine when his wife is barren.[47]

[45] For a statement concerning discovery of the tablets and the light they throw on the Jacob–Laban narrative, see under "Jacob."

[46] Cyrus Gordon, "Biblical Customs and the Nuzu Tablets," *Biblical Archaeologist* (February 1940), p. 2. Though the Nuzu tablets come from the mid-second millennium and thus are later than Abraham, they are usually thought to reflect customs dating hundreds of years earlier.

[47] Ibid., p. 3 and Code of Hammurabi, law 145. The Code of Hammurabi was found by the French archaeologist, M. J. de Morgan, in 1901 at Susa (Iran), whence it was carried by the Elamites about 1200 B.C. when they sacked Babylon. The code is a shaft of black diorite about eight feet high and six feet in circumference at the base. About three hundred laws are written on the monument. Hammurabi originally set up his code in the temple of Marduk in Babylon about 1700. If one dates Abraham earlier than 1700, he can still apply Hammurabi's laws to Abraham's social context because Hammurabi was only a codifier. Lipit-Ishtar of Isin (in Babylonia) produced a code of similar laws about 1850 B.C. And Bilalama at Eshnunna (northeast of Baghdad) produced a somewhat similar code

Moreover, the Code of Hammurabi declared that the handmaid was not to rank with her mistress. And if the handmaid tried to assume such rank, the mistress could "reduce her to bondage and count her among the female slaves."[48] So Sarai was absolutely within her rights in dealing harshly "with Hagar" to the point that the handmaid fled. Apparently Sarai did reduce her to a position of slavery. But Sarai was not within her rights in asking Abraham to cast out Hagar and Ishmael after Isaac was born (Gen. 21:10). Abraham opposed the idea, perhaps not only because of his love for Ishmael but because this was forbidden in the social context of which he was a part. The Nuzu tablets specifically state that a handmaid's offspring was not to be expelled.[49] It took a special revelation from God to persuade Abraham that he should expel the lad and his mother (Gen. 21:12).

THE DESTRUCTION OF SODOM AND GOMORRAH

About twenty years[50] after Abraham rescued Lot and his belongings from the booty wagons of the kings of the East, he found Lot in trouble again. While the people of the cities of the plain owed a great debt to Abraham for his intervention on their behalf (Gen. 14:16–24), they apparently were not willing to worship Abraham's God. Their wickedness, which was great when Lot first came in contact with Sodom (Gen. 13:13), went on unabated. Finally God determined to destroy the cities of the plain as He had the

about 2000 B.C. Prior to Bilalama, similar laws were codified at Ur. These earlier codes are quite incomplete, however; and if one wishes to study the ancient Mesopotamian system of law in any detail, it is necessary to refer to Hammurabi's code.

[48]Code of Hammurabi, laws 145, 146.

[49]Gordon, "Biblical Customs and the Nuzu Tablets," p. 3.

[50]Abraham was seventy-five when he entered Canaan (Gen. 12:4ff.). Soon thereafter Abraham and Lot separated and the Eastern invasion occurred. Apparently Abraham's victory was accomplished some years before he took Hagar as a concubine at eighty-five (Gen. 16:3). He was one hundred when Sodom and Gomorrah were destroyed (Gen. 17:17; 21:5).

generation of Noah (Gen. 18:20–21; 19:13). Through the intercession of Abraham God spared Lot and his family by means of a supernatural warning. Although Lot's wife was turned to salt because of her disobedience, he and his two daughters reached Zoar safely. The other four cities of the plain were destroyed by "brimstone and fire." Ever since that time the destruction of Sodom and Gomorrah has served as a warning to those who engage in gross sin.

Location of the cities. With the development of Palestinian studies during the last century, there has naturally been considerable interest in the location and excavation of the cities of the plain. To date none of these cities has been excavated, but in recent decades there has been considerable agreement on locating them below the surface of the south end of the Dead Sea. Bits of evidence to support such a conclusion are found in various works, but J. Penrose Harland has provided one of the best summaries of the available information.[51]

In the Scripture itself appear several indications leading to the conclusion that Sodom and Gomorrah were in the southern part of the Dead Sea region. Three references are particularly convincing. Genesis 14:10 states that the battle between the four kings and the five was fought in the "vale of Siddim," which was "full of slime pits" or bitumen wells. Bitumen has appeared and does appear in considerable quantities around the Dead Sea, especially around the southern end of it. Second, according to Genesis 19:20–23, Lot escaped from Sodom to nearby Zoar. Albright pointed out that in Roman, Byzantine, and Arabic times there was a town of Zoar located at the south end of the Dead Sea. Since this site bore no evidence of occupation before the Christian Period, Albright believed that the town of Abraham's day now lies under the waters of the Dead Sea and that the name was transferred to the new town.[52] At least the name *Zoar* has long been applied to a town in this region. Third, Genesis 14:3 states that the battle of the four kings and the

---

[51]J. Penrose Harland, "Sodom and Gomorrah, " *Biblical Archaeologist* (May 1942), pp. 17–32.

[52]Albright, *Archaeology of Palestine and the Bible,* p. 135.

five took place in the vale of Siddim, "which is the salt sea." In other words, Harland suggests that this parenthetical clause indicates that the vale of Siddim subsequently was overflowed by the Dead Sea. Josephus[53] confirms the testimony of this biblical reference in saying that with the disappearance of Sodom the valley has become a lake, "the so-called Asphaltitis" (his name for the Dead Sea).

That the water level of the Dead Sea has risen in modern times is confirmed by abundant evidence, not the least of which is the large number of dead trees standing in the water at the south end of the Dead Sea. The road around the southern end of the sea has been under water since the end of the last century. One authority, writing about 1924, claimed that the southern basin had increased by about one-third in the previous century.[54] Moreover, it is now known that a Roman road ran along the east side of the Dead Sea and across El Lisan ("the tongue" that juts out from the eastern shore) to the western shore. So it must have been possible to ride or walk across that area of the Dead Sea in Roman times. Perhaps it should be noted that most of the southern part of the sea is only about twelve to fifteen feet deep and that the water level commonly rises at least two to three inches each year. The sea expands and contracts with climatic conditions, however; and presently it is contracting, partly as a result of the fact that river water flowing into it is being used for irrigation. There are no outlets from the Dead Sea by means other than evaporation.

Many have thought that archaeological confirmation of the location of the cities of the plain under the waters of the Dead Sea was provided by discoveries at Bab edh-Dhra', located just east of El Lisan. This large fortified enclosure was believed to be a religious or festival site for nearby cities. While there were cemeteries and a worship center there, no permanent dwellings appeared. Moreover, the pottery and other artifacts that have been recovered dated from between about 2300 and 1900 B.C. Subsequently the site was unused.

---

[53] *Antiquities* 1, 9.
[54] Harland, "Sodom and Gomorrah," p. 30.

If Bab edh-Dhra' was related to the activities of people of the plain, it would no longer have been needed after the destruction of towns in the area.[55]

In 1959, pilots flying over the area just south of El Lisan reported glimpsing what appeared to be remains of pillars, streets, and houses at the bottom of the Dead Sea. Some have speculated that these ruins might belong to ancient Gomorrah.[56] Subsequently Dr. Ralph E. Baney of Kansas City, Missouri, executive director of the Christian Approach Mission which had an orphanage in Bethlehem, conducted diving operations in the area for about three months, concluding April 28, 1960. He claimed to have found under the southern end of the Dead Sea remains of two cities which he identified as Sodom and Gomorrah, as well as a viaduct, a levee, a road, and other items of lesser significance. Immediate reaction among scholars in the United States ranged from the cautious to the skeptical—pending a checking of details. After studying the explorer's report, the Jordan Antiquities Department declared that Baney had failed to produce evidence of his supposed finds. The department claimed that the viaduct had been built by the American Point Four Program, that the road had been built for the former Palestine Potash Company and was destroyed during the 1948 Palestine war, and that the explorer had failed to produce photographic or material proof of existence of the sunken cities.[57] While in Jordan subsequent to Baney's activities, the writer learned that Baney's claims had been completely discredited.

As a result of more recent developments, Bab edh-Dhra' must be looked at in a new light, and the whole question of the location of the cities of the plain has been reopened. Paul W. Lapp excavated at Bab edh-Dhra' for the American Schools of Oriental Research for three seasons

[55] Albright, *Archaeology of Palestine and the Bible,* pp. 136–37; Harland, "Sodom and Gomorrah," pp. 26–28.

[56] Chicago *Sun-Times,* December 28, 1959, p. 1.

[57] "Find in Dead Sea Linked to Sodom," *The New York Times,* April 29, 1960, p. 33; "Did Not Find Sodom and Gomorrah," *The Muskegon* (Mich.) *Chronicle,* May 11, 1960, p. 11.

during the years 1965 to 1967 and discovered there a town of about ten acres which came to an end, he believed, in the twenty-third century B.C. But tombs in the area continued to be used down into the twenty-second and twenty-first centuries B.C. Presumably the town had some special significance because the cemetery is estimated to hold some 500,000 individual burials.[58] Certainly that many people had not lived in the town itself during its period of occupation.

Some now conclude that the town of Bab edh-Dhra' was destroyed when Sodom was and therefore date that event in patriarchal history about 2300 B.C. But it may be argued that the end of this town's corporate history had nothing to do with the catastrophe of Genesis 18–19 and that instead it was the burials in its cemeteries which ceased after the destruction of Sodom and Gomorrah. If the latter is the case, the cessation of the burials would tally roughly with the Hebrew chronology for Abraham, which would put the destruction of the cities of the plain about 2075 B.C.

Then in 1973, Walter E. Rast and R. Thomas Schaub began an extended exploration of the southern and eastern Ghor and launched excavations at Bab edh-Dhra' and others of the towns discovered in the Ghor. Rast and Schaub have now discovered four additional towns along the eastern edge of the Ghor (five with Bab edh-Dhra'), and they conclude that all of them came to an end about 2350. At least three of them were destroyed by fire.[59]

At the same time that Rast and Schaub were doing their work, the Ebla tablets were making their impact on biblical study (see appendix). Professor Giovanni Pettinato of the Ebla dig announced on October 29, 1976, the appearance of the names Sodom and Gomorrah on one of the Ebla tablets. Since both the Ebla tablets and the end of the cities of the

[58] A. Ben-Tor, "Bab Edh-Dhra'," *Encyclopedia of Archaeological Excavations in the Holy Land,* 1, 149–51.

[59] See William C. van Hattem, "Once Again: Sodom and Gomorrah," *Biblical Archaeologist* (Spring 1981), pp. 87–92; and Walter E. Rast and R. Thomas Schaub, "Preliminary Report of the 1979 Expedition to the Dead Sea Plain, Jordan," *Bulletin of the American Schools of Oriental Research* (Fall 1980), pp. 21–61.

southern Ghor date to about 2350 B.C., some would like to put the events of Genesis 14 and 18–19 that early. And they suggest that the five cities of the plain were not located in the plain at all but along the eastern edge of the Ghor.[60] In developing his thesis to support that view van Hattem argued that the valley of Siddim (1) was only a place near the five cities where their kings chose to do battle (Gen. 14), (2) that it was full of slime or bitumen pits and unfit for agriculture, and (3) that the falling of some into those pits suggests unfamiliarity with the terrain.[61]

All of this hypothesizing requires comment. In the first place, the Ebla tablet as reported did not indicate the destruction of Sodom and Gomorrah; only commercial transactions were involved. The tablet merely confirmed the existence of the two towns. Second, there is no proof that the destruction of the towns along the eastern Ghor had anything to do with the destruction of the cities of the plain of the Jordan. After all, those destructions took place some three hundred years before even the Masoretic (Hebrew) text would place the destruction of Sodom and Gomorrah (c. 2075), and the Masoretic chronology is the earliest of all chronologies of the patriarchal age. A major conflict in the area hundreds of years before Abraham could have resulted in the destruction of those towns. Third, even if one assumes that the towns were not located in the valley, there could be other towns to serve as candidates for some or all of the five cities of the plain. As van Hattem himself has said, a survey of the sort Rast and Schaub are doing on the east side of the Ghor might find remains of other early towns on the west side of it.[62] Fourth, the five towns studied by Rast and Schaub have not been positively identified with any of the biblical towns.

Fifth, the existence of bitumen deposits and some outcroppings of bitumen did not need to have rendered the

---

[60]See, e.g., van Hattem, "Once Again: Sodom and Gomorrah"; and David Noel Freedman, "The Real Story of the Ebla Tablets, Ebla and the Cities of the Plain," *Biblical Archaeologist* (December 1978), pp. 143–64.

[61]Van Hattem, "Once Again: Sodom and Gomorrah," p. 87.

[62]Ibid., p. 90.

whole area sterile. The Genesis text indicates that its general prosperity was very attractive to Lot. Sixth, the fact that some fell into bitumen pits does not necessarily prove general unfamiliarity with the region. It may only indicate that the five kings were so out-generaled and so out-maneuvered that they found themselves with their backs to some of those pits and were pushed into them while trying to escape. Seventh, aspects of this hypothesizing must be altered in light of the conclusion that Sodom and Gomorrah are not mentioned in the Ebla tablets after all. An earlier reading was erroneous.[63]

The whole question of the location of the five cities of Genesis 18 and 19 must be left open. There is still no proof they are not under the southern part of the Dead Sea. Possibly one or more of them will be discovered on the western side of the Dead Sea. As noted, the towns studied by Rast and Schaub have not been positively connected with any of the biblical towns. Moreover, the chronological conclusions of Rast and Schaub need further study. The excavators are having difficulty making carbon-14 and pottery chronology dates for some of the sites jibe; there are unexplainable gaps of one hundred fifty years or more between dates arrived at by these two methods of dating.[64] At least there is general agreement that the five cities must have been somewhere in the vicinity of the southern end of the Dead Sea.

Nature and destruction. The Bible states that God "rained upon Sodom and upon Gomorrah brimstone [literally sulphur] and fire . . . out of heaven" (Gen. 19:24) and that He "overthrew those cities, and all the plain" (Gen. 19:25). An investigation of how God brought about this destruction is facilitated by J. Penrose Harland in a second installment on Sodom and Gomorrah.[65]

---

[63]See James D. Muhly, "Ur and Jerusalem Not Mentioned in Ebla Tablets," *Biblical Archaeology Review* (November/December 1983), pp. 74–75.

[64]Rast and Schaub, "Preliminary Report of the 1979 Expedition to the Dead Sea Plain, Jordan," pp. 46–47.

[65]J. Penrose Harland, "Sodom and Gomorrah," Part Two, *Biblical Archaeologist* (September 1943), pp. 41–54.

Harland calls to our attention observations of the Greek geographer Strabo (end of the first century B.C.) concerning the area at the south end of the Dead Sea. Strabo mentioned ruined settlements, fissures in the ground, ashy soil, scorched rocks, and other evidences of a general destruction in the region. He attributed much of the destruction to earthquakes. Josephus (end of first century A.D.) also described the burned out appearance of the area and remains of ruined cities. Parenthetically it should be observed that, according to the testimony of these men, apparently the land south of El Lisan was not entirely under water by A.D. 100. Writing about the same time, Tacitus attributed, as did Josephus, the destruction of the cities of the plain to bolts of lightning and described the burned out appearance and destruction of the fertility of the land. Some of the ancient writers also spoke of the existence in the plain of asphalt seepages and boiling waters emitting foul odors. Great quantities of asphalt or bitumen appear in the Dead Sea region and continue to rise to the surface of the water.

Harland then reconstructs the story of the destruction as follows, "A great earthquake, perhaps accompanied by lightning, brought utter ruin and a terrible conflagration to Sodom and the other communities in the vicinity. The destructive fire may have been caused by the ignition of gases and seepages of asphalt emanating from the region, through lightning or the scattering of fires from hearths."[66] Harland also quotes extensively from a geological survey of the region by Frederick G. Clapp, who concluded that the "slime pits" were probably oil or bitumen seepages and held to the probability of the existence of natural gas in the area. Clapp further observed that seepages of semifluid petroleum may still be found near the south end of the Dead Sea.[67]

From all this discussion it is clear that there was an abundance of combustible material near the cities of the plain. And there is no reason to doubt the Genesis account of intense fire and smoke and the raining of fiery substance on

[66] Ibid., p. 48.
[67] Ibid., p. 49.

the cities, possibly as a result of gas explosions which threw burning material into the air. Whether lightning touched off fire and explosions or whether earthquakes created a chain reaction need not concern us here. Genesis describes the catastrophe, and early geographers attest to it.

In answer to one who feels that the supernatural has been discounted in the foregoing discussion, it should be observed that miracles do not always involve the avoidance of secondary causes. Moreover, often the time element is the main feature in a miracle. In this case God may have used an earthquake and lightning to set on fire combustible materials, *after adequate warning to Abraham and Lot and after Lot's escape from Sodom and in complete accordance with a divine timetable.*

PALESTINE IN ABRAHAM'S DAY

To understand the age of Abraham in particular and the patriarchs in general, it is necessary to discover what contemporary scholarship has to say about conditions in Palestine during the late third and early second millennia B.C. And Palestinian developments should be placed in the larger context of the Middle East. Before about 2200 B.C. the whole area had entered into an "intermediate period." The Old Akkadian period had ended in Mesopotamia and the hated Guti were in the land. The Old Kingdom had collapsed in Egypt and local governors, or nomarchs, had asserted themselves in the confused times of the First Intermediate Period. In Palestine and much of Syria deurbanization had set in as early as the twenty-fourth century B.C. and certainly characterized the land during the period 2200–2000 B.C.

It used to be claimed that the last centuries of the third millennium B.C. in Palestine represented a major cultural break perpetrated by an invasion of Amorites who wrought great destruction everywhere, bringing urban life to an end. The degree of break in civilization was thought to justify the view that the Early Bronze Age had come to an end and the Middle Bronze Age had begun. Now that view is greatly modified. Evidently there was no major cultural break in

Palestine during the latter part of the third millennium, and the last quarter of the millennium should be designated as Early Bronze IV. Moreover, apparently there was no invasion of Amorites with consequent destruction at the various sites. To be sure, there was general deurbanization throughout Palestine by the end of the twenty-third century, but it is argued that this did not occur as a result of invasion, with the possible exception of a few sites in the south, which suffered Egyptian attack before the fall of the Old Kingdom. Rather, the abandonment of towns resulted from a significant shift to drier conditions combined with a greatly weakened economy and the disruption of trade systems.[68]

Then, gradually at first and later more rapidly, reurbanization of Palestine began during the twentieth century and was completed during the nineteenth. As late as about 2050 B.C. Egyptian rulers showed disdain for the weak Asiatics of Palestine, but shortly after 2000 B.C. Pharaoh Amenemhet I built a line of forts along the eastern frontier to keep check on their movements. Subsequently Egyptian execration texts (curses inscribed against enemies of Egypt) reveal something of the rise of urbanization in Palestine. These curses pronounced against towns and districts of Palestine date to two periods: the end of the twentieth and beginning of the nineteenth centuries, and about the end of the nineteenth century. A large number of Canaanite towns (some mentioned in the Old Testament) and their rulers were cursed. In passing, it is interesting to note that the central and southern hill country of Palestine continued to be rather thinly settled even after the rapid growth of urbanization elsewhere. The new developments that occurred in Palestine after 2000 B.C. represented a real cultural break and ushered in the Middle Bronze Age. It is generally believed

---

[68] See Suzanne Richard, "Toward a Consensus of Opinion on the End of the Early Bronze Age in Palestine-Transjordan," *Bulletin of the American Schools of Oriental Research* (Winter 1980), pp. 5–34.

that an Amorite intrusion had much to do with the political and cultural changes.[69]

In the eighteenth century, apparently, a people known to the Egyptians as Hyksos (meaning "rulers of foreign lands") came to dominate Palestine and much of Syria. Evidence points to the conclusion that these people were essentially Semitic in the earlier days but were somewhat infused with Hurrian and Indo-Aryan elements after the seventeenth century. The Hyksos infiltrated Egypt during the eighteenth century or earlier and were sufficiently numerous there so they were able to take the reins of government in the Nile delta and Lower Egypt from weak native dynasts about 1720 and hold them until the middle of the sixteenth century. Their domination of Upper Egypt lasted for about one hundred years. It is now generally believed that the Hyksos did not have to fight much, if at all, to topple native Egyptian rulers.

The patriarchal period in Palestine fits admirably into the historical context just sketched. If one follows the chronology of the Hebrew text, Abraham would have entered the land just after 2100 B.C., when urban life had virtually ceased and when seminomadism would have been possible. No great cities or city states would have confronted the patriarch. And, as noted, when reurbanization occurred, it was less pronounced in the central and southern hill country, where the patriarchs spent most of their time. Moreover, the Hebrew chronology would put the Israelite entrance into Egypt about 1875, when Asiatic migration into Egypt was getting under way and when Palestine was becoming sufficiently built up into powerful city states as to make seminomadism more difficult there. Utilization of later chronologies for the patriarchal period would place the patriarchs in adverse to impossible circumstances, as far as pastoral seminomadism is concerned.

As Abraham and his entourage moved around in

---

[69] See Yohanan Aharoni, *The Archaeology of the Land of Israel,* Anson F. Rainey, trans. (Philadelphia: Westminster Press, 1982), pp. 81–97; John Bright, *A History of Israel,* 3rd ed. (Philadelphia: Westminster Press, 1982), pp. 54–55.

Palestine, they came in contact with a number of other groups that had also entered the area. Actually, Scripture views all these peoples as Canaanites, as a comparison of Genesis 10:15–19 and 15:19–21 (cf. Deut. 7:1; Exod. 23:23) indicates. But with the passage of time they had become separate groups and had staked out territories for themselves. The mere listing of these groups seems to demonstrate how politically or ethnically fragmentized Palestine was in Abraham's day and how it was therefore possible for him to maintain himself under somewhat hostile circumstances. Brief comments on some of these groups follow.

Canaanites. Canaan, progenitor of the Canaanites, was a son of Ham and brother of Mizraim, progenitor of the Egyptians (Gen. 10:6).[70] Ethnically, as noted, Canaan is viewed as the ancestor of all the peoples Abraham met in Palestine. Geographically, the term applied to the area from Phoenicia south to Gaza and inland to the Dead Sea (Gen. 10:19). Culturally, Canaanite referred to the developments in Egyptian Asia, which were influenced by Egypt but modified by Hyksos, Indo-Iranian, and other contributions. Excavations reveal that Canaanite achievements in architecture, metal and wood working, needlecraft, commerce, and in many other ways were very advanced. But the Canaanites were also a morally debased people, engaging in sex worship and infant sacrifice.[71] This moral degradation became more evident around the middle of the second millennium than it was about 2000 B.C. The term *Canaanite* came to be used in two senses in the Old Testament—referring to the people who lived west of the Jordan or to a tribe inhabiting a particular locality. When used in the latter sense it denoted a

---

[70] In connection with the continuing race question, it is important to observe that the curse of Genesis 9:25 was leveled against Canaan, not Ham. Anyone who has studied Palestinian archaeology knows that the Canaanites were not negroid and that they were a morally debased people. It may be suggested with good reason that now that the Canaanites have passed off the world stage the curse against them has been completely fulfilled and we need not look for contemporary fulfillment.

[71] See Albright, *Yahweh and the Gods of Canaan;* and John Gray, *The Canaanites* (New York: Frederick A. Praeger, 1964).

people settled by the sea and alongside the Jordan—in the lowlands of Palestine (Num. 13:29).

Amorites. Genesis 10:16 indicates that the Amorites were descended from Canaan, but they must have intermarried with Semites very early because they appear as a Semitic people in Near Eastern references to them. Their origin is something of a mystery, but they probably arose not too far from the Syro-Palestine region, perhaps in the northern Euphrates area. Their language was one of the Northwest Semitic dialects and thus closely related to Canaanite and biblical Hebrew.

The Amorites began to appear in southern Mesopotamia before 2500 B.C. By 2000 B.C. they had mingled with the native Mesopotamians and had founded several city states. Mari was one of the most powerful of these. Amorites also became the ruling dynasty of the Old Babylonian Kingdom; Hammurabi was of Amorite stock. In Syria they established kingdoms at Aleppo, Alalakh, and elsewhere. After 2000 B.C. they appeared in force in Palestine, and from certain artistic representations it may be concluded that they were entering Egypt as traders by 1900 B.C. Presumably they formed an important element in the Hyksos development.

In the Old Testament the term sometimes refers to the inhabitants of Palestine generally (Gen. 15:16; Judg. 6:10). Similarly the Amarna tablets (Egyptian, fourteenth century B.C.) refer to the entire area of Palestine and Syria as *Amurru* (land of the Amorites). Sometimes in the Old Testament the Amorites are said to occupy the hill country, while the Canaanites lived in the lowlands of Palestine. Occasionally Amorites are spoken of as a specific people under a king of their own. For example, during the patriarchal period they appeared as a power on the western shore of the Dead Sea (Gen. 14:7), at Hebron (Gen. 14:13), and at Shechem (Gen. 48:22). Later the Amorites occupied an area in Transjordan as well as in Canaan. Numbers 21:21 speaks of Sihon, king of the Amorites, and Joshua 10:5 lists the towns of the Amorite league: Jerusalem, Hebron, Jarmuth, Lachish, and Eglon. The Amorites developed a fairly advanced culture, especially demonstrating craftsmanship in gold, silver, bronze, and leather; and they were very successful in commercial activities and administrative efficiency.

Philistines. Both Abraham (Gen. 21:22–32) and Isaac (Gen. 26:15) had dealings with the Philistines. But such an assertion creates problems for the Bible student because biblical critics commonly have thought the Scripture to be in error at this point. It is generally recognized that Ramses III of Egypt repelled a Philistine invasion from Crete shortly after 1200 B.C. and that the Philistines then settled near the sea in southern Palestine. But it is not generally recognized that Philistines may have occupied the area as early as 1900 or 2000 B.C. To deal with this problem, it is necessary to note that the Old Testament says the Philistines came from the island of Caphtor (Jer. 47:4; Amos 9:7), commonly identified as Crete. Moreover, the term *Cherethites* (Cretans) is used to designate the Philistines in Ezekiel 25:12; Zephaniah 2:5; and 1 Samuel 30:14.

If the Philistines of about 1200 B.C. came from Crete, they would have been part of the warlike maritime culture known as Mycenean or else of the Sea Peoples who were pushed out of the Aegean by the Mycenean Greeks. And in Palestine they were warlike and a constant threat to the Israelites during the days of Judges and early monarchy. This later development is extensively documented by archaeological discovery. No earlier stage of Philistine presence has turned up in Palestinian excavations, however; and there lies the problem.

By way of solution it should be noted, first, that Minoan Cretans were establishing trading colonies around the Mediterranean by about 2000 B.C., and evidence of their contact with Palestine and Egypt during this early period is substantial. Moreover, the Philistines of Abraham's day were peace-loving agricultural people, as were the Minoans. Second, G. Ernest Wright has pointed out that the Hebrew word translated "Philistine" was used for all "Sea Peoples," of whom the Philistines were the most important for the inhabitants of Palestine.[72] Possibly the reference in Genesis

---

[72] G. Ernest Wright, "Philistine Coffins and Mercenaries," *Biblical Archaeologist* (September 1959), p. 61.

should be translated by some other term. Finally, it should be noted that the Gerar of Abimelech (Gen. 21, 26) has now been identified with Tell Abu Hureira, about eleven miles southeast of Gaza. In 1956, D. Alon excavated there and found that it was inhabited continually through every period from Chalcolithic times to the Iron Age and was very prosperous during the Middle Bronze (the patriarchal) Age. He also found several smelting furnaces, giving evidence of Philistine iron working.[73] So some evidence of the culture of which Abimelech was a part has been found, but the name "Philistine" has not been connected with it.

Hittites. According to the patriarchal narrative, when Sarah died, Abraham bought from a Hittite a field in which was located a cave suitable for burial purposes (Gen. 23:7; 25:9–10). Critics commonly treat this reference to Hittites as an anachronism later inserted by an editor or by a historian who made a mistake. It is thought not to reflect historical conditions during Abraham's lifetime. The problem is that the Old Hittite Kingdom in Asia Minor (modern Turkey) did not exist until about 1650 B.C., and Hittite remains in Syria and Palestine (even those recovered in recent excavations) do not date before the thirteenth century B.C. When the Hittite kingdom did exist, it did not extend its authority into southern Palestine. So it would seem to be in error to conclude that Abraham may have met them there about 2000 B.C.

A possible solution to the problem may be found in a better understanding of Hittite history. When scholars began to excavate Hittite towns and to recreate history, they found themselves working with a language and culture that was Indo-European in character. Of course this was dubbed "Hittite." Then it was discovered that long before the Indo-European developments a non-Indo-European culture had

[73] Edward E. Hindson, *The Philistines and the Old Testament* (Grand Rapids: Baker, 1971), p. 72. See also Trude Dothan, *The Philistines and Their Material Culture* (New Haven, Conn.: Yale University Press, 1982); N. K. Sandars, *The Sea Peoples* (London: Thames and Hudson, 1978); and D. J. Wiseman, ed., *Peoples of the Old Testament Times* (Oxford: Clarendon Press, 1973).

existed in Hittite land. But now that the term *Hittite* had been specifically assigned, those people could not be called Hittites. Actually, discoveries reveal that several rather prosperous non-Indo-European states had come into existence in Asia Minor during the third millennium B.C. Then Indo-European peoples came into Asia Minor either from the northwest or the northeast long before 2000 B.C. and gradually made their way across the peninsula. Apparently they reached the Hittite heartland and subdued its inhabitants about the middle of the nineteenth century B.C. And it took another two centuries before the invaders established the Old Hittite Kingdom. The "Proto-Hittite" element remained as a sub-stratum in the society.

The suggested solution to the problem is that some of the "Proto-Hittite" non-Indo-European sons of Heth (Gen. 10:5) may have found their way to Palestine and settled in the Hebron area as part of the larger Canaanite culture. As noted, the Proto-Hittites of the third millennium B.C. had developed rather prosperous states in Asia Minor and some of them were involved in rather extensive and far-flung commercial activities. It is not out of line to speculate that citizens of these states may have found their way into Palestine and had dealings with Abraham. It is not necessary to conclude that the Bible is in error in alluding to Hittites in Palestine in Abraham's day.

Harry Hoffner, professor of Hittite studies at the University of Chicago, does not believe that the Hittites of the patriarchal period had any connection with the "Proto-Hittites," but he does not deny the historical validity of the Genesis references. He observes that the Hittites of the patriarchal period had good Semitic names (rather than the Indo-European of the northern Hittites) and concludes that their customs did not diverge greatly from those of their Palestinian neighbors. He simply classifies them as another group that could validly be called "Hittites" in ancient times.[74]

---

[74]H. A. Hoffner, "The Hittites and Hurrians," in *Peoples of Old Testament Times,* D. J. Wiseman, ed. (Oxford: Clarendon Press, 1973), pp. 213–14.

6 | *ISAAC*
Genesis 25:19–28:5

BEERSHEBA

Just as Abraham fell out with the Philistines over water rights in thirsty southern Palestine, so did his son Isaac. Just as Abraham made a covenant of peace with the Philistines at Beersheba, so did Isaac. At the time of their conflict with the Philistines, both patriarchs worshiped at Beersheba, too. And at the same site God confirmed the Abrahamic covenant to Isaac (Gen. 21:22–34; cf. Gen. 26:14–33). On these and numerous other occasions Beersheba figured prominently in the history of the Hebrew people.

A millennium and a half before Abraham and Isaac, civilization had reached a fairly high point of development in the Beersheba area, as excavations have shown. From 1951 to 1960 Jean Parrot led a French archaeological mission dig at prehistoric sites near Beersheba. They worked at Beer Matar, about a mile southeast of Beersheba, from 1951 to 1954, and at nearby Beer Safad for five seasons. Then in 1952 and 1954 Moshe Dothan excavated at Horvat Batar, another site in the vicinity, on behalf of the Israel Department of Antiquities.

These villages were peculiar in that they were built

underground, at least in the early phases, sometimes at a depth of six yards or more, with access by vertical shafts or sloping tunnels. The rooms of the houses generally measured about ten by fifteen or ten by twenty feet. The culture of these villagers reached a high degree of development for such an early time, and the villagers were not without their comforts. They raised cattle and at least three kinds of grain, kept several kinds of domesticated animals, made agricultural tools and weapons, and engaged in several handcrafts— including pottery making and manufacture of objects of stone, bone, and ivory. The copper industry was quite highly developed there, too. Since there were no copper ores in the vicinity, the smith had to travel more than sixty miles to tap the rich deposits south of the Dead Sea.[1]

The culture of the Beersheba area was closely related to that of other towns located between the Mediterranean coastal plain and the south end of the Dead Sea. When, a little after 3000 B.C., the Beersheba culture declined as a result of factors not yet fully determined, the culture of the other towns did, too. For the next millennium, life in the Negev was almost completely nomadic, and attempts at civilized settlement were unsuccessful. The picture changed, however, during the twenty-first century B.C. when the Negev again was dotted with villages, as archaeological surveys in the area show. Of course Beersheba benefited from this new spurt of prosperity to the south. When Abraham first entered the area it was enjoying a period of peace and prosperity, which was to last for some two hundred years. Thereafter another millennium was to elapse before the Negev again enjoyed a period of prosperity. While Beersheba's development was affected greatly by what happened in the Negev to the south, it always remained important as a meeting and market place. The biblical narrative clearly demonstrates that significance.

The biblical town of Beersheba has been located at Tel es-Saba (Tell Beersheba), about two miles northeast of the

---

[1] See Nelson Glueck, *Rivers in the Desert* (Philadelphia: Jewish Publication Society, 1959), pp. 39ff.; and "Beersheba" in *Encyclopedia of Archaeological Excavations in the Holy Land,* 1:153–58.

modern city. Yohanan Aharoni directed a Tel Aviv University excavation there from 1969 to 1976. He discovered that the town had a Hebrew foundation, built in the twelfth and eleventh centuries B.C. Apparently unwalled, it probably was the place where the sons of Samuel judged the people (1 Sam. 8:2). Beersheba was fortified with a twelve-foot-thick wall in the tenth century. At that time the enclosed area was a little less than three acres in size. The details of the excavation are not pertinent to the present study because they concern the monarchy rather than the patriarchal period.

Aharoni found nothing at Tell Beersheba dating to the patriarchal period, and he concluded that patriarchal Beersheba was located near the valley and the wells, probably at Bir es-Saba, within the area of modern Beersheba.[2] Ze'ev Herzog, reporting on the last three seasons of excavation at Tell Beersheba, describes efforts to dig below the twelfth century level to see if anything of the patriarchal era could be found. Though they dug to bedrock, the excavators uncovered nothing earlier than 1250 B.C. habitation, aside from a few fourth millennium sherds. Herzog now inclines to the view that the patriarchal age should be moved to the thirteenth or twelfth century B.C.[3] Of course that is chronologically impossible. Herzog observed that some scholars have used evidence from Beersheba to support the position that there was no patriarchal age and that the patriarchal accounts were composed during the monarchy to create a history for the state.[4] Such an extreme view is totally unwarranted in the light of all that archaeology has done to vindicate the antiquity and authenticity of the patriarchal tradition. But John Bright (himself no friend of historical or textual inerrancy of the Bible) warns that on the one hand archaeology "has not proved that the stories of the patriarchs happened just as the Bible tells them." It cannot do that. But

---

[2] Yohanan Aharoni, "Tel Beersheba," *Encyclopedia of Archaeological Excavations in the Holy Land,* 1:160–68.

[3] See Ze'ev Herzog, "Beer-sheba of the Patriarchs," *Biblical Archaeology Review* (November/December 1980), pp. 12–28.

[4] Ibid., p. 26.

on the other hand, "No evidence has come to light contradicting any item in the tradition."[5] It is to be admitted that excavations at Tell Beersheba have presented a problem, but Aharoni's suggestion that patriarchal Beersheba may have been within the confines of modern Beersheba serves as a temporary solution.

From Beersheba the road leads almost due eastward to Kir-haresheth, capital of Moab. From there one can make his way southward to the land of Edom with its almost legendary capital at Petra. Genesis declares "Esau is Edom" (36:8) and indicates that Esau went to live there after his estrangement from Jacob (33:16). Since the days of Edom's greatness did not come until several centuries after the patriarchal period, and since the days of Petra's climb to fame did not begin until about the time of Nebuchadnezzar, the territory is not discussed here.

THE ORAL BLESSING

The immediate event that led to the estrangement of Jacob and Esau was Jacob's theft of the oral blessing from his brother. When Isaac was old and blind and fearful of imminent death, he called his elder son to him to receive a blessing. Before Isaac bestowed the blessing, however, he wanted another meal of wild game which Esau must have frequently furnished. Rebekah overheard the conversation between Isaac and Esau and instigated the deception by which Jacob stole his brother's blessing. Isaac, finally persuaded that Jacob was Esau, blessed him, saying, "Be lord over thy brethren, and let thy mother's sons bow down to thee" (Gen. 27:29). Hardly had the aged father finished when Esau came in from the hunt and claimed the blessing. Isaac, distraught over what had happened, did not simply observe that a mistake had been made and switch the blessing to its rightful owner. Nor did Esau ask him to do so. Admitting he had lost the right to receive the chief

    [5]John Bright, *A History of Israel,* 3rd ed. (Philadelphia: Westminster Press, 1981), p. 75.

blessing, he merely asked for some sort of additional blessing from his father. To a modern Occidental this passage is puzzling. Why wasn't the mistake rectified, we ask?

Before answering, we should try to discover what this phenomenon really was. Near the end of his life, Jacob blessed Ephraim and Manasseh in the same way as Isaac had blessed his sons (Gen. 48). Shortly thereafter, on his deathbed, Jacob called all his sons for a blessing before he died. On that occasion headship of the family was bestowed on Judah, even though he was not the oldest son (Gen. 49:8). It seems clear from a study of these accounts that the oral blessing was given by an aged or dying father to his sons and that it was an oral will.

From excavations at Nuzu (Nuzi) in central Mesopotamia we learn that the oral blessing or will had legal validity and would stand up even in the courts. Nuzu tablet P56 mentions a lawsuit between three brothers in which two of them contested the right of a third to marry a certain Zululishtar. The young man won his case by arguing that this marriage was provided for in his father's deathbed blessing.[6]

Against such a background, it is easy to understand why the oral blessing was so important and why a father, once having bestowed it, could not revoke it. In a patriarchal society without the elaborate probate machinery that we possess, adequate safeguards were necessary to ensure the execution of a will of a testator. Since literacy was low in the society of which Isaac and Jacob were a part, an oral blessing would take on great significance.

It should be noted that while the Nuzu tablets date to the fifteenth century B.C., they reflect customs and social

---

[6]Cyrus Gordon, "Biblical Customs and the Nuzu Tablets," *The Biblical Archaeologist* (February 1940), p. 8. See also M. J. Selman, "Comparative Customs and the Patriarchal Age," *Essays on the Patriarchal Narratives,* ed. by A. R. Millard and D. J. Wiseman (Winona Lake, Ind.: Eisenbrauns, 1983), pp. 91–139. He shows in this chapter the need for caution in dealing with Nuzi material but is generally quite positive in accepting its contribution to biblical study.

conditions of northern Mesopotamia and Syria dating centuries earlier. Some of these customs continued on into the late second millennium B.C. or even into the first millennium. Evidently they were established practices in the society from which the patriarchs came in Mesopotamia and with which they maintained contact during the days when Jacob lived there.

7 | *JACOB*
Genesis 25:24–49:33

THE PURCHASED BIRTHRIGHT

Jacob did a good job of living up to his name (which means "supplanter"), at least during the early years of his life.[1] Even before he stole Esau's blessing, he managed to win his inheritance. One day as Esau came in from hunting, ready to drop from weariness and hunger, Jacob took advantage of him by refusing to serve him a meal until Esau gave up his birthright (inheritance) in exchange for it (Gen. 25:29–34). Although certainly the sale of one's birthright was not a common practice in Bible lands, it is interesting to note that archaeological discovery has provided a parallel to this story. Again the Nuzi tablets provide the example.

---

[1] Often the question is asked why God would bless such a rogue as Jacob. It almost seems as if He put His stamp of approval on sin. It should be remembered that God never chose followers for what they were but for what they could become by His grace. The story of Jacob's life should not be looked upon as an account of God's blessing on wickedness but rather as an account of God's patient dealing with a sinful man until he became Israel, "fighter for God," or "striver with God." His new name bears out the tenacity and perseverance of his character. Jacob was not without punishment either. For example, he was exiled from home for twenty years, himself a victim of deception.

N204 tells about a certain Tupkitilla who gave his inheritance rights in connection with a grove to his brother Kurpazah in exchange for three sheep. It is not clear exactly why Kurpazah was able to drive such a hard bargain, but it seems that he took advantage of some extremity of his brother. Perhaps this extremity was hunger; perhaps Tupkitilla was a dissolute character who wanted to throw a banquet for his friends and did not have the means to do so.[2]

THE JACOB–LABAN CONTEST

After Jacob robbed Esau of his blessing, he found it safer to leave home than to stay. His mother sent him to her brother Laban in Haran (in northwestern Mesopotamia). At last Jacob met his match; Laban outwitted him at almost every turn.

The clay tablets of Mesopotamia have thrown considerable light on social relationships of the patriarchal period. Cyrus Gordon cites one of the Nuzu[3] tablets (G51) which he believes closely parallels the Jacob–Laban narrative. Because his interpretation is so convincing, and because it contributes so much to the understanding of the biblical account, an extended summary is provided here. First it is necessary to give a translation of tablet G51.

> The adoption tablet of Nashwi son of Arshenni. He adopted Wullu son of Puhishenni. As long as Nashwi lives, Wullu shall give (him) food and clothing. When Nashwi dies, Wullu shall be the heir. Should Nashwi beget a son, (the latter) shall divide equally with Wullu but (only) Nashwi's son shall take Nashwi's gods. But if there be no son of Nashwi's, then Wullu shall take

---

[2] Cyrus Gordon, "Biblical Customs and the Nuzu Tablets," *The Biblical Archaeologist* (February 1940), p. 5.

[3] Excavations at Nuzu were carried on in 1925–31 by the American School of Oriental Research at Baghdad under the direction of Edward Chiera. During the course of the excavation thousands of clay tablets were found in private homes, business houses, and the palace. Dating to the fifteenth century B.C. these tablets tell a great deal about social relationships similar to those appearing in the patriarchal narratives in Genesis and therefore shed light on the interpretation of several biblical passages.

Nashwi's gods. And (Nashwi) has given his daughter
Nahuya as wife to Wullu. And if Wullu takes another
wife, he forfeits Nashwi's land and buildings. Whoever
breaks the contract shall pay one mina of silver (and) one
mina of gold.

Gordon suggests that the relationship of this tablet to
Scripture will become clear if "Laban" is substituted for
"Nashwi" and "Jacob" for "Wullu."

The interpretation would then run something like this.
Laban adopted Jacob (at least he made him a member of his
household) and made him heir, sealing the transaction by
giving Jacob a daughter to be his wife. As long as Laban
lived, Jacob had the responsibility of caring for him. When
Laban died Jacob would inherit Laban's estate in full if Laban
failed to have any sons. If Laban had natural sons, each
would receive an equal share of the property, and one of
them would receive the household gods, which signified
headship of the family.

How did this arrangement work out in the biblical
narrative? Laban seems to have adopted Jacob, giving him
two daughters to wife. When Jacob ran away, Laban
claimed, "These daughters are my daughters, and these
children are my children, and these cattle are my cattle, and
all that thou seest is mine. . . ." (Gen. 31:43). Laban asserted
absolute authority over Jacob and all his family and belongings, a right he would have had if Jacob was adopted. Later it
seems that sons were born to Laban. (Twenty years elapsed
between the time Jacob came to Laban and his flight from
Laban's household, Gen. 31:41.) Laban's natural sons began
to feel that Jacob took away their inheritance, and after the
sons were born Laban's attitude toward Jacob changed (Gen.
31:1–2). When the friction became unbearable, Jacob and his
family determined to flee. As they fled, Rachel made off with
the family gods, which would have given family headship to
Jacob instead of the natural sons of Laban. When Laban
caught up with the escapees, he was particularly concerned
about the images. It is quite likely that Rachel had no interest

in the idols for their religious value but sought them for social prestige they would bring to her husband and herself.[4] We need not insist that this very appealing interpretation be accepted, but the biblical narrative certainly makes much more sense when viewed in its social context.

The Nuzi texts are not the only materials available to provide information on the social context of the Jacob–Laban narrative. Parallels to practices reflected at Nuzi appear at Mari, Alalakh, Ugarit, and elsewhere. The herding practices and marriage contracts of ancient Mesopotamia and Syria are similar throughout the second and first millennia B.C.[5] The agreements of Jacob and Laban resemble Old Babylonian herding contracts of the eighteenth century B.C. and follow principles enunciated in the Code of Hammurabi (see especially laws 261–267), as Morrison has shown.[6] Records of lawsuits supplement the actual contracts. Jacob's contracts to work as a herdsman for Laban in return for specified wages and Jacob's protests concerning his good service (Gen. 36:36–39), e.g., repayment of loss caused by wild animals, bear similarities to Old Babylonian materials. Morrison has also shown that in Old Babylonian and Nuzi materials and in Genesis, shearing time was the "focal point of the herding cycle." That event in the spring was the time when accounts were settled and contracts drawn up for the coming year. Moreover, she observes that Jacob's departure from Laban was at the time of shearing of sheep (Gen. 31:19), at the end of the contract period. So he could leave honorably, having completed obligations for the previous year but not yet having assumed any for the coming year.[7]

[4]Gordon, "Biblical Customs and the Nuzu Tablets," pp. 5–7. See also James B. Pritchard, ed., *Ancient Near Eastern Texts Relating to the Old Testament* (Princeton: Princeton University Press, 1955), pp. 219–20.

[5]Martha A. Morrison, "The Jacob and Laban Narrative in Light of Near Eastern Sources," *Biblical Archaeologist* (Summer 1983), pp. 155–64.

[6]Ibid., p. 156; cf. Pritchard, *Ancient Near Eastern Texts Relating to the Old Testament*, p. 177.

[7]Ibid., p. 158.

8 | *JOSEPH*

Genesis 37:2–50:26

THE TIME OF JOSEPH'S ENTRANCE
INTO EGYPT

In discussing the time when Abraham lived, we have already given considerable attention to the chronology of the patriarchal period. At that point it was observed that according to the chronology in the Hebrew Old Testament, Jacob and his sons may have entered Egypt about 1875 B.C. If one follows the Septuagint (Greek) version of the Old Testament, he will arrive at a date of approximately 1800 B.C. for the entrance of the Israelites into Egypt. Acceptance of a late date for the Exodus and a figure of 430 years (Exod. 12:40) for the Hebrew sojourn in Egypt would place their entrance into Egypt about 1700 B.C.

The writer has tended to accept the 1875 B.C. date. But this poses a real problem. Would Joseph have been able to rise to great power in Egypt under a native dynasty? Or would his relatives have been readily permitted to settle in the land at this early date? Supposedly foreigners were not welcome in Egypt before the seventh century B.C. Such was the claim of Greek and Roman writers, and higher critics have accepted their testimony.[1] Archaeological confirmation of the entrance of foreigners into Egypt during the patriarchal period has been found in the tomb of Knumhotep, who lived at Beni Hasan, 168 miles south of Cairo. A painting in his tomb depicts a visit by thirty-seven Asiatics (Semites) of the desert bringing gifts and desiring trade. The date of the visit has been fixed at 1892 B.C.,[2] certainly earlier than the earliest possible date for the entrance of Jacob and his sons.

But there is much more than the pictorial representation from Knumhotep's tomb to support the early entrance of foreigners into Egypt. Apparently the Hyksos began to infiltrate the eastern delta during the nineteenth century B.C. So if we take an early date for the entrance of the Hebrews into Egypt, they would have come in during the period of Hyksos infiltration—when many foreigners were apparently entering. If we accept a date of about 1700 or 1650 B.C. for the entrance of the Hebrews, the Hyksos would have been ruling Egypt and likely would have received other foreigners. This introduces the question of who the Hyksos were and what their relation to the Hebrews was.

Manetho, an Egyptian historian who lived about 250 B.C., introduced the name Hyksos and said that it meant "shepherd kings." This terminology has stuck until recently. Now it is known that *Hyksos* really meant "rulers of foreign lands" and that the Egyptians generally referred to the Hyksos as *Aamu,* meaning "Asiatics." This still does not specify who the Hyksos were. Hitti spoke of them as "a horde, an unclassified goulash of humanity which the melting pot of the eastern Mediterranean had spilled over the edge and washed down into Egypt."[3] He continued by observing that among them were Semites and non-Semitic

[1] Joseph P. Free, *Archaeology and Bible History,* 2nd ed. (Wheaton, Ill.: Scripture Press, 1956), pp. 53–54.

[2] Jack Finegan, *Light From the Ancient Past,* 2nd ed. (Princeton: Princeton University Press, 1959), pp. 92–93.

[3] Philip K. Hitti, *History of Syria* (New York: Macmillan, 1951), p. 146.

peoples—including Hurrians (biblical Horites), Hittites, and possibly several other minor peoples.[4] The predominant element among them was Semitic. At the height of their power the Hyksos controlled the Delta of Egypt and much of southern Egypt, all of Palestine, and at least part of Syria. They left extensive remains at various biblical sites, e.g., Hazor.

While the Egyptians, who hated the Hyksos, preferred to think of their invaders as uncultured barbarians, archaeological and historical studies have demonstrated that the Hyksos actually contributed much to Egyptian culture. They introduced the horse and chariot (the ancient equivalent of a tank as far as psychological effects are concerned), a new type of sword, and the composite bow. They were skillful metal smiths, jewelers, and pottery-makers. Many scholars give them credit for introducing the art of inlay in bone or ivory.

In addition to the possibility that Joseph and his relatives may have entered Egypt during the period of Hyksos rule, there are at least three other connections between the Hyksos and the biblical narrative. First, it is clear that the Egyptians did not consider the Hebrews to be part of the Hyksos movement. When the native Egyptians drove out their foreign overlords in the sixteenth century B.C., the expulsion did not involve the Hebrews. Second, it may well be that the rise in Egypt of a king who did not know Joseph (Exod. 1:8) really signifies the rise of a native Egyptian dynasty, which would not have been sympathetic with the Hebrews. One would not expect the Egyptians to be very sympathetic with a foreign element that came in during Hyksos days. The resurgent nationalism of the period would certainly have resulted in opposition to the Hebrews. Third, the fact that the Hyksos brought the horse into Egypt is intimated in the Bible. Genesis 47:17, which refers to Joseph's receiving horses in payment for food, is the first biblical reference to horses. Regardless of the date of Joseph's entrance into

---

[4]Ibid.

Egypt, he would have been there contemporary with at least some of the Hyksos.

JOSEPH AS PRIME MINISTER OF EGYPT

A crisis disturbed the Egyptian palace. Pharaoh had a dream and was convinced that it had some special meaning (Gen. 41:1–13). But none of his spiritual or political advisers could give him any counsel concerning it. Finally the chief butler remembered a young Semitic slave who had correctly interpreted his dream while the butler was in prison for some malfeasance of office. This Hebrew, Joseph by name, was brought from prison to counsel the Pharaoh. Attributing to God the wisdom he had for interpreting dreams, Joseph explained that the seven fat cows that Pharaoh saw coming up out of the Nile signified seven years of plenty in Egypt. The seven lean cows that came out of the river and devoured the fat ones indicated seven years of famine that would consume the prosperity of the good years. Joseph admonished the king to choose a capable administrator for all Egypt and store 20 percent of the produce during each of the good years so that there would be enough during the famine.

Pharaoh was impressed that Joseph was just the man for the job. He apparently made Joseph grand vizier or prime minister—the second in command in the nation. Pharaoh gave Joseph as symbols of office his official ring, put a gold chain or collar around his neck, and gave him an official chariot in which to ride, preceded by a herald who would announce his coming (Gen. 41:40–44).

Critics used to doubt the possibility of a Palestinian slave's rising to such high position in Egypt as Scripture says Joseph did. But archaeological investigation has provided several interesting parallels to this occurrence. A Canaanite, Meri-Ra, became armor-bearer to Pharaoh; another Canaanite, Ben-Mat-Ana, was appointed to the high position of interpreter,[5] and Yankhamu, a Canaanite (possibly of He-

---

[5] S. L. Caiger, *Bible and Spade* (London: Oxford University Press, 1951), p. 61.

brew origins) seems to have been the Egyptian governor of Palestine at the beginning of the reign of Akhenaton or Amenhotep IV.[6]

The biblical statement of Pharaoh's promotion of Joseph to high position is in accord with known Egyptian court proceedings for formal installation of a prime minister over Egypt.[7] The ring was engraved and was used for the purpose of stamping soft materials (such as sealing wax) with the king's seal in order to give a document official status—much in the same way that a notary public's seal makes a document official today. The gold chain or collar was a mark of distinction among Egyptian officials.

That Joseph was promoted to the position of prime minister seems to be confirmed by an inscription telling about the duties of a certain Antef, prime minister of the Pharaoh. The inscription describes Antef as the "functionary of the signet [ring] . . . chief of the chiefs . . . alone in the multitude, he bears the word to men; he declares all affairs in . . . Egypt; he speaks on all matters in the place of secret counsel.[8]

Joseph was favored by God with divine wisdom and by Pharaoh with the royal prerogative and the arrangement of a marriage alliance with the most powerful religious leader in the land. Joseph was, therefore, in an incomparable position as the second officer in all of Egypt. However, it must not be thought that Joseph necessarily compromised his religious convictions because he married the daughter of the high priest of On. It is clear from the ensuing chapters of the biblical narrative that he remained faithful to the God of his fathers and to his Hebrew family ties. His dying words prophesied God's removal of the children of Israel from Egypt, and he elicited a promise that his body would be carried along when they left (Gen. 50:22–26).

---

[6] James B. Pritchard, ed., *Ancient Near Eastern Texts Relating to the Old Testament,* 2nd ed. (Princeton: Princeton University Press, 1954), p. 486.

[7] I. M. Price, O. R. Sellers, and E. Leslie Carlson, *The Monuments and the Old Testament* (Philadelphia: Judson Press, 1958), p. 161.

[8] Ibid., pp. 161–62.

EGYPT, LAND OF PLENTY—THE FAMINE

It is often said that Egypt is the Nile. And how true that is! Were it not for the Nile, the country would be a vast desert—as is the adjacent territory of North Africa. Along the Mediterranean, rainfall is about eight to twelve inches, while at Cairo it approximates only one to two inches a year. Rain occurs even less frequently to the south.

In addition to furnishing water for irrigation, personal needs, and cattle, the Nile indirectly provided clothing for the Egyptians because flax, from which linen is produced, was among the crops raised. Moreover, the river provided a highway for the people; from very early times small boats for travel only, as well as large transport barges, have plied the Nile waters. To demonstrate further that Egypt is the Nile, one should take note of the fact that the verdant area of the country stretches in a narrow line along the river, varying from about one to ten miles. From clay along the banks of the Nile Egyptians made pottery and formed bricks for construction purposes. Because the Nile was so important to Egyptian life it was deified and worshiped as Hapi.

At its mouth the Nile formed a delta, as have the Tigris and Euphrates and other great rivers of the world. This pie-shaped section is about 125 miles north and south and 115 at its greatest width. In flowing through the delta, the Nile split up into many branches, most of which have now silted up—leaving the Rosetta and Damietta as the two most important streams. Along the eastern edge of the delta lay the land of Goshen, where the children of Israel lived during their sojourn in Egypt. This area of grassland was especially useful to the Hebrews, who were primarily a pastoral people rather than agricultural.

"The Nile Valley was a tube, loosely sealed against important outside contact."[9] Egypt was protected on the north by the Mediterranean; she did not suffer a major invasion from that quarter until the twelfth century B.C.—and that was repulsed. Egypt was protected on the east and

[9]John A. Wilson, *The Burden of Egypt* (Chicago: University of Chicago Press, 1965), p. 11.

west by the desert; because the eastern frontier proved to be penetrable, an ancient "Maginot Line" was constructed there. From the south the six cataracts of the Nile served as barriers to invasion. These were rough places or rapids (between Aswan and Khartoum) where the river cut unevenly through its rocky bed. The cataracts were more than mere inconveniences to mariners. For instance, the fifth cataract is 100 miles in length, and the river bed drops more than 80 feet in that distance. the fourth cataract is 80 miles long and has a drop of 110 feet. All of this protection kept Egypt free from the constant invasion that Mesopotamia and Palestine suffered all during their history.

The White Nile begins south of the equator (some 2,500 miles from the Mediterranean) and winds northward over a stream bed about 4,000 miles in length. The area around its source is watered by almost daily tropical rains, ensuring a constant volume of water. After a distance of about 1,600 miles, the White Nile is joined by the Blue Nile, which drains the Abyssinian highlands. About 150 miles farther north the Atbara flows into the Nile. The annual flood of the Nile is caused by the waters of the Blue Nile and the Atbara. The latter is an insignificant stream except at flood season; the former dumps a tremendous volume of water into the Nile during the Abyssinian rainy season. Before the completion of the first Aswan Dam in 1902, the annual flood of the Nile began in June and crested in September and October. Thereafter there was a gradual decline in water level, and the fields dried off by the end of March and were ready for cultivation.

The flood of the Nile deposited a layer of rich silt over the land and mixed in a generous supply of humus— vegetation brought downstream from tropical areas. Moreover, it watered and softened the land and left behind substantial quantities of water in reservoirs which the Egyptians constructed to trap water needed for irrigation purposes. A rise of the river about twenty-five or twenty-six feet at Aswan meant a normal inundation. A thirty-foot Nile would sweep away dikes and canal banks and destroy the mud-brick villages. A high Nile thirty inches below normal meant a hard year; a high Nile sixty inches below normal meant famine.[10] So precariously was Egypt perched on the banks of the Nile. Of course the Nile did not always behave perfectly.

This discussion of the Nile and its habits and significance in Egyptian life has been introduced in order to provide background for comments on the famine in Joseph's time. That a famine of such magnitude could and did occur in Egypt is indicated by an Egyptian inscription dating during the reign of Ptolemy X, about 100 B.C. This refers to a famine of seven years' duration which occurred during the reign of King Djoser, about 2700 B.C. The text tells how Djoser appealed to the god Knum for help and in the process told about the great lack of food, wholesale robbery produced by the extremity of human need during the famine, the physical weakness of the people who did not have enough to eat, and the perplexity of the court now that the public storehouses had been emptied of all reserves.[11] Obviously this famine took place many hundreds of years before the time of Joseph, but it does demonstrate the existence of extended famine.

There are several references in Egyptian inscriptions to disastrous famines and to the feeding of hungry petitioners. But it is hard to connect any of these with the Joseph narrative with any degree of certainty. Brugsch has assigned one of these famines to the time of Joseph. It seems that a certain Baba of El-Kab did for his city what Joseph is said to have done for all Egypt. He prepared for a famine of several years' duration and then distributed food to the people during the famine. The inscription concludes as follows: "I collected corn as a friend of the harvest-god. I was watchful in time of sowing. And when a famine arose, lasting many years, I distributed corn to the city each year of famine."[12] Baba lived about 1500 B.C. It should be observed that Brugsch has not been generally followed, but his suggestion

[10]Ibid., pp. 10–11.

[11]G. A. Barton, *Archaeology and the Bible,* 7th ed. (Philadelphia: American Sunday-School Union, 1937), pp. 370–71.

[12]Ibid., p. 371.

is an interesting possibility. If one accepts Brugsch's view, Baba would probably have been one of the many local officials who collected grain under the direction of Joseph. It seems, however, that this famine is too late to have any connection whatsoever with Joseph. About the most that can be said is that Baba may have copied the technique of Joseph in preparing for famine.

At any rate, it seems that the famine of Joseph's day affected far more than the Nile Valley, for Joseph's brethren came down to Egypt from Palestine to buy grain.

It is interesting now to try to place Joseph, his administrative duties, and the entrance of his people in the context of Egyptian history. Acceptance of the Hebrew chronology would place the entrance of Jacob and his extended family into Egypt in about 1876 B.C. At that time Sesostris III (or Senwosret or Sen-Usert) would have been ruling. Though Egyptian chronologies vary, most would conclude that Sesostris's regnal dates were 1878 to 1840 B.C. If these dates are right, the seven years of plenty and the beginning of Joseph's administration would have occurred during the reign of the previous Pharaoh, Sesostris II (1897–1878). The Bible student will discover no evidence of a change of royal administration in the Genesis narrative, and many think therefore that the wrong Egyptian historical context has been suggested for Joseph's ministry. But as crown prince, Sesostris III presumably would have acquiesced to the policies inaugurated by his father. And he would have been king when the years of famine set in. An alternate view, choice of a chronology that puts the regnal years of Sesostris III at 1887–1850, would envision him as in full control during the entire period of Joseph's leadership in Egypt.

It is not enough to identify the Pharaoh of the famine years. We are curious about what was going on in Egypt at the time and whether it is possible that Joseph's activity is reflected in the historical situation. By way of answer it should be noted that when the Egyptian Middle Kingdom began, the political structure was quite feudalistic. That is to say, the nomarchs or governors of the forty-two administrative districts of Egypt often operated fairly independent of the crown, and the Pharaoh had comparatively little coercive power. The Pharaohs tried to reverse the situation and made some progress. But progress was particularly great during the reign of Sesostris III. In fact, by the time he died, feudalism was largely gone. He may even have abolished the office of nomarch. This achievement could have been related to Joseph's use of the famine, no doubt under the Pharaoh's direction, to fasten royal control on all the populace of the land (see Gen. 47:13–26). Sesostris III was a very vigorous Pharaoh and one of the most renowned kings in the ancient history of Egypt. He pushed the southern frontier about two hundred miles south of Aswan, to the second cataract, and reconquered Nubia. He also cut a canal through the first cataract of the Nile at Aswan to promote commerce and communication and continued the land reclamation project of his father in the Fayum area.

EMBALMING IN ANCIENT EGYPT

After Jacob died, Joseph gave orders for the physicians to embalm his father. They took forty days to complete the process, and Jacob was mourned for seventy days. When Joseph died he also was embalmed according to the practice of the Egyptians (Gen. 50:2–3, 26). This immediately raises the question of how the Egyptians embalmed or mummified their dead.

The whole subject of mummification has suffered from much misinformation. Many of those who have studied the subject and written on it have depended too much on observation and speculation and not enough on chemical analysis of mummy wrappings and the like. One of the most valuable studies on mummification is by A. Lucas, former director of the Chemical Department of Egypt and Honorary Consulting Chemist of the Department of Antiquities of Egypt.[13] The viewpoint espoused here is largely based on the work of Lucas.

[13] A. Lucas, "Mummification," in his *Ancient Egyptian Materials and Industries,* 3rd ed. (London: Edward Arnold, 1948), pp. 307–90.

In earliest Egypt mummification was not practiced, but because the sands beyond the area of cultivation were so dry in most of the land, bodies are still found in a good state of preservation. When mummification was introduced is unknown but it was certainly commonly practiced by around 2500 B.C. and continued on into the early Christian era. For many centuries only members of the royal family, nobles, priests, high officials, and the wealthy were embalmed.

In trying to preserve the body, the Egyptians obviously sought to remove the liquid, about 75 percent of the body weight. This could be done either by natural or artificial heat (a practice that proved to be impracticable) or by use of a dehydrating agent. Three such agents which the Egyptians might have used were quick lime, common salt, and natron (native carbonate of soda). Lucas demonstrates that quick lime was not used in ancient Egypt before the Greek period and that salt, apart from that contained as an impurity in natron, was not used in mummification. Rather the Egyptians always used natron because it was regarded as a purifying agent and because it chemically destroyed fat.

The best and almost the only ancient writers describing the process of mummification are Herodotus and Diodorus. Lucas has shown that some of the misconceptions regarding mummification are based on mistranslations of the Greek in these writers. (One of the most common of these misconceptions is that the body was embalmed by soaking it in salt brine for an extended period of time.) Lucas observes that both writers compare the process of preserving the body to the process of preserving fish—namely salting; but Herodotus states that the agent used to preserve the body was natron. In other words, the practice was to dry out the body over an extended period of time by means of continued application of natron. Lucas supports his interpretation of Herodotus by means of histological studies made on Egyptian mummies and concludes, "The evidence from the pathological examination of mummies, therefore, furnishes no justification for thinking that the bodies were soaked in a bath or solution, but it all points in the opposite direction."[14] Just how the natron was applied is not known, but it has been found frequently tied up in small parcels in linen cloth and sometimes is found mixed with sawdust, which could serve as an additional absorbent.

While the procedure differed with different periods, different places, and the social status of the person to be embalmed, certain generalizations regarding mummification can be made. First, the organs were customarily removed through an incision in the left side, with the exception of the heart and kidneys, which remained in place. These organs were separately treated and placed in four stone containers known as "canopic jars." These jars were sealed and had their lids carved to represent the heads of gods. The brain was usually not removed until during the eighteenth dynasty (about 1570–1300 B.C). Obviously, in Jacob's and Joseph's time the practice was to leave the brain in place. Next the abdominal and chest cavities were washed with palm wine and spices.[15]

Then the body was treated with natron—for forty days according to the Genesis account; but the process might last as long as seventy days. When the body was ready for burial it was washed with a natron bath and anointed with cedar oil and other ointments. It was customary to stuff the chest and abdominal cavities with linen soaked in resin. Occasionally these cavities were left empty. Then the body was wrapped with endless yards of linen strips soaked in resin, and often resin was poured over the mummy when it was partially wrapped. Finally the body was placed in a painted wooden coffin inscribed with religious formulae. This is probably fairly close to the procedure employed in the embalming of the patriarchs. In succeeding centuries it became common to place thimbles over the fingers to hold the nails in place, to

---

[14]Ibid., p. 326.

[15]As Egyptian embalmers worked in such detail with bodies over extended periods of time, they became quite expert in aspects of anatomy and were therefore better equipped to perform operations and to engage in other forms of medical practice.

fill out the body by inserting packing between the skin and bones, and to paint the outside of the wrapped mummy.

So it was in this mummified condition that Jacob's body was taken by Joseph to be buried in Palestine. And it was in this condition that Joseph's body was carried out of Egypt at the time of the Exodus. But hundreds of years were to elapse before the corpse was to accompany the children of Israel out of Egyptian slavery to the land promised as an everlasting possession to their great forebear Abraham, father of the faithful.

APPENDIX

Some Excavations Significant for the Study of Genesis and Archaeology

BETHEL

Bethel, twelve miles north of Jerusalem, was the place where Abraham pitched his tent and built his first Palestinian altar (Gen. 12:6–8) and where Jacob had his dream of angels ascending and descending a ladder and pledged his loyalty to God (Gen. 28:10–22; 35:6–7). W. F. Albright began work at Bethel (modern Beitin) in 1927. He was able to work only on the north side of the ancient mound because the modern village covers the southern part of the city. In 1934 Albright returned to work at the site, with J. L. Kelso of Pittsburgh–Xenia Theological Seminary as assistant. Professor Kelso returned to Beitin to excavate in 1954, 1957, and 1960. Work at the site demonstrates that the city was established as a Canaanite settlement about 3200 B.C. but was unoccupied during much of the Early Bronze Age. Reoccupied c. 2400–2200, it was again abandoned for a couple of centuries. Then about 2000 B.C. the continuous occupation of the site began—destined to end only with the Muslim occupation of Palestine in the seventh century A.D. Of course, various destructions occurred along the way, e.g., by the Egyptians in the sixteenth century B.C., the Israelites in the thirteenth century, and Nebuchadnezzar in 587 B.C. If one follows the Masoretic chronology of the Old Testament, Abraham would have built his altar there in the twenty-first century when the site was uninhabited. The city became an important center for calf worship during the administration of Jeroboam I, about 930 B.C. See J. L. Kelso, "Bethel," *Encyclopedia of Archaeological Excavations in the Holy Land*, 1:190–93; and W. F. Albright and J. L. Kelso, "The Excavation of Bethel (1934–60)," *Annual of the American Schools of Oriental Research* 39 (Cambridge, Mass., 1968).

BOGAZKÖY

While several important excavations have been conducted in Hittite territory, at such places as Sinjerli (1889–91) and Carchemish (1911ff.), the most important expedition worked at Bogazköy (now officially Bogazkale, Hittite Hattusha) in north central Asia Minor (modern Turkey). This was the capital of the ancient Hittite Empire. Professor Hugo Winckler of Berlin began work there in 1906 and had the singular good fortune to discover almost immediately the record office of the Hittite capital—still containing over ten thousand tablets. These documents were written in several languages, some of which cannot yet be translated. Winckler led the German Oriental Society dig at Bogazköy from 1906 to 1912, excavating and mapping the walls, the gates, and the major temples. Then in 1931 Kurt Bittel assumed leadership of the excavation, which continued annually until 1939 and resumed in 1952. The German excavations continue to the present but have only begun to uncover the massive 400-acre site. See O. R. Gurney, *The Hittites*, rev. ed. (Baltimore: Penguin Books, 1961); and J. G. Macqueen, *The Hittites* (Boulder, Colo.: Westview Press, 1975).

DOTHAN

Dothan was the town near which Joseph was put in a pit by his brothers and later sold into slavery. It is located about ten miles north of Samaria. Cistern pits like the one into which Joseph was thrown may still be seen nearby. Professor Joseph P. Free of Wheaton College (Illinois) conducted excavations at the site for nine seasons between 1953 and 1964. He discovered eleven layers indicating occupation ranging between 3000 B.C. and A.D. 1400. Excavation on top of the mound reached the town of Elisha's day (Elisha was here when the Assyrians surrounded the town, 2 Kings 6:15, and were smitten with blindness), but the excavation has touched the level of Joseph's time only in areas down the slope of the mound. The great find of the 1959 season was the richest tomb yet found in Palestine. Used from 1400 to 1100 B.C., it contained more than 3,200 pottery vessels.

EBLA (TELL MARDIKH)[1]

The best publicized and the most controversial excavation currently being conducted in the Middle East is that of ancient Ebla (Tell Mardikh), located about thirty miles south of Aleppo. A University of Rome team under the direction of Paolo Matthiae has been working on the 140-acre mound since 1964. Excavations reveal that the city enjoyed its greatest era between about 2400 and 2250 B.C. but that it enjoyed another period of power and prosperity between 2000 and 1600 B.C.

Of special significance among the finds at Ebla are about twenty thousand clay tablets and fragments of tablets, nearly all dating from the earlier period. These are written in cuneiform but are mostly in the Eblaite language, which is Semitic and has affinities with biblical Hebrew. Though decipherment is in its infancy and few texts have been published, some categorization has been attempted. About 80 percent are thought to be economic; the rest are lexical or linguistic, literary, historical, and juridical.

In the early days of assessment of the Ebla tablets Giovanni Pettinato was chief epigrapher of the Italian Mission to Ebla, and he made numerous claims linking Ebla to the Bible. These were sensationalized and widely reported and commented on in the popular press and in scholarly journals, especially in the United States. Connections with the Bible ranged from alleged discovery of fragments of a creation story to the mention of Sodom and the other cities of the plain, to the appearance of names of Jerusalem and other Palestinian sites.

Then as a result of a personal and scholarly dispute with Matthiae, Pettinato cut his ties to the Italian Ebla Mission, and Alfonso Archi of the University of Rome's Institute of Near Eastern Studies was named new chief epigrapher. Since 1979 Archi has been refuting the views of Pettinato relative to biblical connections with the Ebla tablets. The debate between the two epigraphers sometimes has been acrimonious.[2]

In the spring of 1983 members of the Italian Expedition,

---

[1] Three books on Ebla now available are Chaim Bermant and Michael Weitzman, *Ebla* (New York: Times Books, 1979); Paolo Matthiae, *Ebla* (Garden City, N.Y.: Doubleday, 1981); Giovanni Pettinato, *The Archives of Ebla* (Garden City, N.Y.: Doubleday, 1981).

[2] See especially Giovanni Pettinato, "Ebla and the Bible," *Biblical Archaeologist* (Fall 1980), pp. 203–16; and Alfonso Archi, "Further Concerning Ebla and the Bible," *Biblical Archaeologist* (Summer 1981), pp. 145–54.

including Matthiae and Archi, toured the United States for about six weeks. In their lectures they denied that the Ebla tablets, at least as far as is now known, make any reference to Jerusalem, Megiddo, Lachish, Shechem, Sodom, and the other cities of the plain, or Palestine or Egypt in general. Ebla was a Syrian site and the texts focus on inner Syria.[3]

The layperson and scholar alike must accept the conclusions of the scholars who are doing the work on the Ebla texts and wait for new groups of the tablets to be published. If one denies all the sensational claims, however, the significance of Ebla does not disappear. Discoveries there contribute greatly to an understanding of the early history of Syria and the political and economic history of the whole region of the Fertile Crescent during the Early and Middle Bronze ages. Moreover, it is to be remembered that the origins of the patriarchs go back to Ur and Haran and thus to the same general cultural horizon as Ebla. What may be learned from the latter will provide general contextual information for the biblical narrative. At the least, some light on the social and legal aspects of the patriarchal period may be provided by discoveries at Ebla. And the tablets illustrate beyond question the high degree of literacy and civilization in the area long before the patriarchs.

MARI

Mari (Tell Hariri) is located on the Euphrates fifteen miles north of the present Syria–Iraq border. W. F. Albright in 1932 suggested with some confidence that Tell Hariri was ancient Mari. André Parrot of the Louvre led excavations at the site for several months each winter during the years 1933–38 and 1951–56. The history of Mari was discovered to date back to about 3200 B.C.

Most dramatic of the finds at the site were the royal palace and the royal archives of the early second millennium B.C. The palace boasted about three hundred rooms, courts, and corridors, and covered more than eight acres. The walls are still standing to a height of fifteen to twenty feet, and the pottery drains still worked after 3,500 years of neglect.

More important to biblical study, however, were the royal archives, containing upwards of twenty thousand clay tablets. These tablets consist of royal correspondence from many kingdoms of Western Asia and a large number of business documents,

---

[3]See James D. Muhly, "Ur and Jerusalem Not Mentioned in Ebla Tablets," *Biblical Archaeology Review* (November/December 1983), pp. 74–75.

nearly three-fourths coming from the latter category. These tablets have contributed important new information which has modified our knowledge of the chronology of the second millennium B.C. They also provide much new information about the Amorites and therefore about the patriarchal period. The names Peleg, Serug, and Nahor (Gen. 11:16, 22, 24, 27) appear as names of towns in the Mari tablets. Moreover, the tablets mention customs reflected in the patriarchal narrative and throw light on the tribal organization and the traditions of Syria in patriarchal times. See A. Parrot, "Mari," *Archaeology and Old Testament Study*, D. Winton Thomas, ed. (Oxford: Clarendon Press, 1967).

NINEVEH

The location of Nineveh was positively identified in 1847 as the result of excavations by A. H. Layard. Subsequent and very fruitful work was carried on there in the last century by Layard, Hormuzd Rassam, and George Smith for the British Museum and Victor Place for the French. Further expeditions were sent to Nineveh by the British Museum in 1903–5, led by L. W. King and R. C. Thompson, and in 1931–32, under the direction of M. E. L. Mallowan.

While the earlier excavators concentrated on the Great Assyrian Period, Mallowan conducted a prehistoric sounding in the lower levels of the site. At present, Nineveh is represented by two great mounds—Kouyunjik and Nebi Yunus (the prophet Jonah), and the site is so large that it may never be completely excavated. Most of the archaeological work in the past has been conducted at Kouyunjik, where Layard uncovered the palace of Sennacherib and his library.

Another tremendous discovery at the mound was the palace of Ashurbanipal (a success of Rassam) with its royal library. This is one of the most important finds of antiquity because of the number of texts in the library that are related to biblical study, such as Babylonian accounts of creation and the Flood. Moreover, these tablets (copies of Assyrian, Sumerian, and Akkadian materials) provide a key to the understanding of the whole Mesopotamian civilization. The total number of tablets brought to the British Museum from the Assyrian imperial library (as housed in the palaces of Sennacherib and Ashurbanipal) is in excess of twenty-five thousand and represents over ten thousand texts. Ruins of other palaces found on Kouyunjik include those of Tiglath-pileser I, Ashurnasirpal II, and Sargon II. Under the mound of Nebi

Yunus lies the palace of Esarhaddon, but since a modern town is located atop the tell, excavations have been very incomplete.

NIPPUR

Nippur, some fifty miles southeast of Babylon, was an important Sumerian site. The Sumerians lived in Babylonia before the Babylonians. The first excavations at Nippur were conducted by the University Museum of Philadelphia and the Babylonian Exploration Fund in 1889–1900. Leadership was provided by J. P. Peters, H. V. Hilprecht, and J. H. Haynes. In 1948 excavations resumed at Nippur, with the Oriental Institute as the chief sponsoring institution. Successive directors have been D. E. McCown, R. C. Haines, J. Knudstad, and McGuire Gibson. Gibson directed the Institute's fifteenth season there in 1981–82.

The city was a great religious and commercial center, dedicated to the earth god Enlil, who was at the head of the Sumerian pantheon. The principal structures of the city (180 acres in size) include the Enlil temple and its ziggurat (128 by 190 feet) and the great temple to his consort Inanna, the "Queen of Heaven." To the south of this group of religious structures lay what is now known as the Scribal Quarter. There about forty thousand clay tablets have now been found, including economic, religious, and literary texts. Among the religious texts important for biblical study were the Sumerian creation and flood accounts and the Sumerian King List, which mentions long-lived patriarchs and a flood.

NUZI (NUZU)

Excavations were begun at this northeast Iraq site (modern Yorghan Tepe) in 1925 by the American Schools of Oriental Research in Baghdad, under the direction of Edward Chiera, and were continued until 1931. Harvard, the University Museum of Philadelphia, and other institutions cooperated in the continuing operation. Of particular significance was the discovery of about twenty thousand clay tablets in Nuzian private homes, dating to about 1500 B.C. and reflecting customs that had been practiced for centuries in northern Mesopotamia and Syria. These reveal striking parallels to the Jacob–Laban narrative, to the sale of the birthright and the oral blessing. Moreover, it should be pointed out that the Nuzians of the mid-second millennium B.C. were Hurrians, the long-lost Horites of the Old Testament. But Nuzi had a long and illustrious history. Centuries earlier its inhabitants were Semites.

UGARIT (RAS SHAMRA)

Excavations at ancient Ugarit (modern Ras Shamra, about twenty-five miles south of the mouth of the Orontes River) have ranked high in biblical significance. A library of religious texts found near temples to Baal and Dagon, palace archives dealing with financial, legal, and diplomatic affairs, and records from homes of leading citizens have opened new vistas on Old Testament study. These thousands of texts in seven languages written in five scripts date mostly to the fifteenth through the thirteenth centuries B.C.

Of special interest and most numerous in the archives were materials written in an alphabetic script of thirty letters now known as Ugaritic. Closely related to biblical Hebrew, Ugaritic provides knowledge of the latter at the time of Moses, when Evangelicals believe the Pentateuch was composed. Ugaritic studies have enabled some previously misunderstood words in the Old Testament to be defined and the meaning of others made clearer. References in Ugaritic tablets to a certain Ura and its merchants have led Cyrus Gordon and others to suggest a northern Ur as the home of Abraham and a merchant-prince association for the patriarch. A study of similarities between Pentateuchal ritual and that of the inhabitants of ancient Ugarit is not germane to the purposes of this book on Genesis.

Claude F. A. Schaeffer began excavations at Ugarit and led eleven campaigns at the site between 1929 and 1939. Resuming work in 1948, he led the excavations there until his thirty-first season in 1969. Several others directed seasons there between 1971 and 1976, and Marguerite Yon of the University of Lyons, France, was appointed director in 1978. Useful new works on Ugarit are Peter C. Craigie, *Ugarit and the Old Testament* (Grand Rapids: Eerdmans, 1983); and Gordon D. Young, ed., *Ugarit in Retrospect* (Winona Lake, Ind.: Eisenbrauns, 1981). See also a major section, "Remembering Ugarit," in *Biblical Archaeology Review*, September/October, 1983.

UR

The site was unknown until 1854, when J. E. Taylor identified al-Muqayyar, about 150 miles north of the Persian Gulf, as Ur. He excavated there briefly, finding a few inscriptions of

Nabonidus, co-ruler of Babylon with Belshazzar at the time the city fell to the Persians in 539 B.C.

In 1918, R. Campbell Thompson began work there under the auspices of the British Museum, to be followed later in the same year by an expedition led by H. R. Hall, representing the same institution. The main work at the site, however, was done by a joint expedition of the University Museum of Philadelphia and the British Museum in a protracted excavation headed by Sir C. Leonard Woolley (1922–34). Woolley discovered the now famous royal tombs, dating to about 2500 B.C. and revealing that a very highly developed culture (Sumerian) existed at that time.

Of more interest to the biblical student are the material remains of the golden age of Ur (2070–1960 B.C. or possibly earlier), which is often considered to be the time of Abraham. The period is well documented with tens of thousands of clay tablets recording bills of lading, invoices, letters of credit, court cases, tax records, and practice tablets of school boys. Remains of the city wall were found, as were remains of dwellings (some of the middle-class homes having ten to twenty rooms), and the great brick ziggurat or stage-tower crowned with a temple to the moon-god Nannar. The flood layer found at Ur also created great excitement. Preeminently, the excavations at Ur introduced to the world the advanced Sumerian civilization and provided a cultural backdrop for the life of Abraham.

SELECTED BIBLIOGRAPHY

Aharoni, Yohanan. *The Archaeology of the Land of Israel.* Trans. by Anson F. Rainey. Philadelphia: Westminster Press, 1982.

Albright, William F. *Archaeology of Palestine and the Bible.* Cambridge, Mass.: American Schools of Oriental Research, 1974.

_____. *Yahweh and the Gods of Canaan.* Garden City, New York: Doubleday, 1968.

Avi-Yonah, Michael, ed. *Encyclopedia of Archaeological Excavations in the Holy Land.* Englewood Cliffs, N. J.: Prentice-Hall. 4 vols. Vol. 1, 1975; Vol. 2, 1976; Vol. 3, 1977; Vol. 4, 1978.

Barton, George A. *Archaeology and the Bible.* 7th ed. Philadelphia: American Sunday-School Union, 1937.

Blaiklock, Edward M., and Harrison, R. K., eds. *The New International Dictionary of Biblical Archaeology.* Grand Rapids: Zondervan, 1983.

Bright, John. *A History of Israel.* 3rd ed. Philadelphia: Westminster Press, 1981.

Bromiley, Geoffrey W., ed. *International Standard Bible Encyclopedia.* Grand Rapids: Eerdmans, Vol. 1, 1979; Vol. 2, 1982.

Caiger, Stephen L. *Bible and Spade.* London: Oxford University Press, 1951.

Finegan, Jack. *Light From the Ancient Past.* 2nd ed. Princeton: Princeton University Press, 1959.

Free, Joseph P. *Archaeology and Bible History.* 2nd ed. Wheaton, Ill.: Scripture Press, 1956.

Glueck, Nelson. *Rivers in the Desert.* Philadelphia: Jewish Publication Society, 1959.

Gray, John. *The Canaanites.* New York: Frederick A. Praeger, 1964.

Heidel, Alexander. *The Babylonian Genesis.* 2nd ed. Chicago: University of Chicago Press, 1951.

————. *The Gilgamesh Epic and the Old Testament Parallels.* 2nd ed. Chicago: University of Chicago Press, 1949.

Hindson, Edward E. *The Philistines and the Old Testament.* Grand Rapids: Baker, 1971.

Kenyon, Kathleen. *Archaeology in the Holy Land.* 3rd ed. London: Ernest Benn, 1970.

Kitchen, Kenneth A. *Ancient Orient and Old Testament.* Downers Grove, Ill.: InterVarsity Press, 1966.

————. *The Bible in Its World.* Downers Grove, Ill.: InterVarsity Press, 1977.

Negev, Avraham, ed. *Archaeological Encyclopedia of the Holy Land.* London: Weidenfeld and Nicolson, 1972.

Parrot, André. *Abraham and His Times.* Philadelphia: Fortress Press, 1962.

————. *The Flood and Noah's Ark.* New York: Philosophical Library, 1955.

————. *The Tower of Babel.* New York: Philosophical Library, 1956.

Pfeiffer, Charles F. *Old Testament History.* Grand Rapids: Baker, 1973.

Price, I. M.; Sellers, O. R.; and Carlson, E. L. *The Monuments and the Old Testament.* Philadelphia: Judson Press, 1958.

Pritchard, James, B., ed. 2nd ed. *Ancient Near Eastern Texts Relating to the Old Testament.* Princeton: Princeton University Press, 1954.

————. *Ancient Near East in Pictures Relating to the Old Testament.* Princeton: Princeton University Press, 1954.

————. *Archaeology and the Old Testament.* Princeton: Princeton University Press, 1958.

Schoville, Keith. *Biblical Archaeology in Focus.* Grand Rapids: Baker, 1978.

Thomas, D. Winton, ed. *Archaeology and Old Testament Study.* Oxford: Clarendon Press, 1967.

Thompson, John Arthur. *The Bible and Archaeology.* 3rd ed. Grand Rapids: Eerdmans, 1982.

Unger, Merrill F. *Archaeology and the Old Testament.* Grand Rapids: Zondervan, 1954.

Vos, Howard F. *Archaeology in Bible Lands.* Chicago: Moody Press, 1977.

————. *Genesis.* Chicago: Moody Press, 1982.

Wiseman, D. J. *Illustrations From Biblical Archaeology.* Grand Rapids: Eerdmans, 1958.

————, ed. *Peoples of Old Testament Times.* Oxford: Clarendon Press, 1973.

————. *The Word of God for Abraham and To-day.* Glasgow: Pickering and Inglis, 1959.

Woolley, C. Leonard. *Ur 'of the Chaldees.'* Rev. by P. R. S. Moorey. London: Hubert Press, 1982.

INDEX